Hebrews
James

ABOUT THE AUTHORS

General editor:

Clinton E. Arnold (PhD, University of Aberdeen), professor and chairman, department of New Testament, Talbot School of Theology, Biola University, Los Angeles, California

Hebrews:

George H. Guthrie (PhD, Southwestern Baptist Theological Seminary), Benjamin W. Perry professor of Bible, school of Christian studies, Union University, Jackson, Tennessee

James:

Douglas J. Moo (PhD, University of St. Andrews), Blanchard professor of New Testament, Wheaton College Graduate School, Wheaton, Illinois

Zondervan Illustrated Bible Backgrounds Commentary

Hebrews
James

George H. Guthrie
Douglas J. Moo

Clinton E. Arnold   *general editor*

ZONDERVAN

Hebrews to James
  Hebrews—Copyright © 2002 by George H. Guthrie
  James, 2 Peter, Jude—Copyright © 2002 by Douglas J. Moo

Requests for information should be addressed to:
Zondervan, 3900 *Sparks Dr. SE, Grand Rapids, Michigan 49546*

This edition: ISBN 978-0310-52307-9

The Library of Congress cataloged the original edition as follows:
  Zondervan illustrated Bible backgrounds commentary / Clinton E. Arnold, general editor.
    p.cm.
  Includes bibliographical references.
  ISBN 978-0-310-27824-5
  1. Bible. N.T. — Commentaries. I. Arnold, Clinton E.
  BS2341.52.Z66 2001
  225.7 — dc21   2001046801

All Scripture quotations, unless otherwise indicated, are taken from The Holy Bible, *New International Version®, NIV®.*
Copyright © 1973, 1978, 1984 by Biblica, Inc.® Used by permission. All rights reserved worldwide.

All rights reserved. No part of this publication may be reproduced, stored in a retrieval system, or transmitted in any
form or by any means — electronic, mechanical, photocopy, recording, or any other — except for brief quotations in
printed reviews, without the prior permission of the publisher.

Interior design by Sherri L. Hoffman

CONTENTS

Introduction vi

List of Sidebars viii

List of Charts viii

Index of Photos and Maps ix

Abbreviations xi

Hebrews 2
    George H. Guthrie

James 86
    Douglas J. Moo

Credits for Photos and Maps 120

INTRODUCTION

All readers of the Bible have a tendency to view what it says through their own culture and life circumstances. This can happen almost subconsiously as we read the pages of the text.

When most people in the church read about the thief on the cross, for instance, they immediately think of a burglar that held up a store or broke into a home. They may be rather shocked to find out that the guy was actually a Jewish revolutionary figure who was part of a growing movement in Palestine eager to throw off Roman rule.

It also comes as something of a surprise to contemporary Christians that "cursing" in the New Testament era had little or nothing to do with cussing somebody out. It had far more to do with the invocation of spirits to cause someone harm.

No doubt there is a need in the church for learning more about the world of the New Testament to avoid erroneous interpretations of the text of Scripture. But relevant historical and cultural insights also provide an added dimension of perspective to the words of the Bible. This kind of information often functions in the same way as watching a movie in color rather than in black and white. Finding out, for instance, how Paul compared Christ's victory on the cross to a joyous celebration parade in honor of a Roman general after winning an extraordinary battle brings does indeed magnify the profundity and implications of Jesus' work on the cross. Discovering that the factions at Corinth ("I follow Paul . . . I follow Apollos . . .") had plenty of precedent in the local cults ("I follow Aphrodite; I follow Apollo . . .") helps us understand the "why" of a particular problem. Learning about the water supply from the springs of Hierapolis that flowed into Laodicea as "lukewarm" water enables us to appreciate the relevance of the metaphor Jesus used when he addressed the spiritual laxity of this church.

My sense is that most Christians are eager to learn more about the real life setting of the New Testament. In the preaching and teaching of the Bible in the church, congregants are always grateful when they learn something of the background and historical context of the text. It not only helps them understand the text more accurately, but often enables them to identify with the people and circumstances of the Bible. I have been asked on countless occasions by Christians, "Where can I get access to good historical background information about this passage?" Earnest Christians are hungry for information that makes their Bibles come alive.

The stimulus for this commentary came from the church and the aim is to serve the church. The contributors to this series have sought to provide illuminating and interesting historical/cultural background information. The intent was to draw upon relevant papyri, inscriptions, archaeological discoveries, and the numerous studies of Judaism, Roman culture, Hellenism, and other features of the world of the New Testament and to make the results accessible to people in the church. We recognize that some readers of the commentary will want to go further, and so the sources of the information have been carefully documented in endnotes.

The written information has been supplemented with hundreds of photographs, maps, charts, artwork, and other graphics that help the reader better understand the world of the New Testament. Each of the writers was given an opportunity to dream up a "wish list" of illustrations that he thought would help to illustrate the passages in the New Testament book for which he was writing commentary. Although we were not able to obtain everything they were looking for, we came close.

The team of commentators are writing for the benefit of the broad array of Christians who simply want to better understand their Bibles from the vantage point of the historical context. This is an installment in a new genre of "Bible background" commentaries that was kicked off by Craig Keener's fine volume. Consequently, this is not an "exegetical" commentary that provides linguistic insight and background into Greek constructions and verb tenses. Neither is this work an "expository" commentary that provides a verse-by-verse exposition of the text; for in-depth philo-logical or theological insight, readers will need to have other more specialized or comprehensive commentaries available. Nor is this an "historical-critical" commentary, although the contributors are all scholars and have already made substantial academic contributions on the New Testament books they are writing on for this set. The team intentionally does not engage all of the issues that are discussed in the scholarly guild.

Rather, our goal is to offer a reading and interpretation of the text informed by what we regard as the most relevant historical information. For many in the church, this commentary will serve as an important entry point into the interpretation and appreciation of the text. For other more serious students of the Word, these volumes will provide an important supplement to many of the fine exegetical, expository, and critical available.

The contributors represent a group of scholars who embrace the Bible as the Word of God and believe that the message of its pages has life-changing relevance for faith and practice today. Accordingly, we offer "Reflections" on the relevance of the Scripture to life for every chapter of the New Testament.

I pray that this commentary brings you both delight and insight in digging deeper into the Word of God.

Clinton E. Arnold
General Editor

LIST OF SIDEBARS

Hebrews

Hebrews: Important Facts. 3
A String of Old Testament Passages Bearing Witness to
    Christ's Superiority (1:5–14) 13
Salvation. 17
Moses 22
Great High Priest 29
Psalms of Righteous Suffering. 33
What Jews in the Greco-Roman Era Thought About Melchizedek. 43
The Heavenly Tabernacle in Judaism 48
How the "New Covenant" Was Understood at Qumran 50
The Tabernacle. 52
The Jerusalem Temple 57
What Is Faith? 68
The Discipline of a Father in the Ancient World. 74
Hospitality in the Ancient World 79

James

James: Important Facts 87
Was James Writing Against Paul's Teaching on Justification
    By Faith Alone? 101
Two Ways of Understanding "Justify": Paul and James 102
First-Century Jewish Moral Teaching 106
The Problem With Wealth 112

LIST OF CHARTS

Men Named "James" in the New Testament 88

INDEX OF PHOTOS AND MAPS

altar
　　of burnt offering (tabernacle), 45, 59
　　of incense (model), 54
anchor, 42
animals, sacrificial, 61
arch, of Constantine, 6
Ark of the Covenant, 51, 55, 64
athlete, 74

bit, 104
boat (*see* ship)
breastplate of high priest, 49
bullae (*see* seals)

Capernaum, synagogue at, 4
Claudius, 8
coins
　　depicting a man with a crown, 18
　　gold, 80
　　with image of Nero, 7
Colosseum (Rome), 6, 9
crown, 18, 74
curtain (in the tabernacle), 64
Dead Sea Scrolls, Temple Scroll, 62

emperors
　　Claudius, 8
　　Nero, 7, 8

fig tree, 105

Galilee, Sea of, 94
goats, 58
grapevine (*see* vines)

harvest, 39, 114
Hercules, 20, 64
high priest (artistic representation), 31, 49

inscriptions
　　House of David, 28
　　Rosetta Stone, 70
incense
　　altar of (model), 54
　　Golden Bowls of (model) 53

jars, 116
Jordan, 87

key, 98

lampstand (*see* menorah)

magical papyrus, 102
manuscript (*see* papyrus; scroll)
menorah, 53
miqveh, 36
mirror, 96
Moses, 22
Mount Sinai, 77

Nero, 7, 8
net, 94

ostracon
　　Greek writing exercise, 34
　　receipt for delivery of a slave, 21

papyrus, magical, 102
potsherd (*see* ostracon)
priest (*see* high priest)

receipt for slave purchase, 21
ring, 98
road, Roman, 6
Rome
　　Arch of Constantine, 6
　　Colosseum, 6, 9
　　Tiber River, 2–3
　　Trajan's Column, 110
　　Via Sacra, 6
Rosetta Stone, 70

scroll, Dead Sea, 62
seals, 12
ship, merchant, 16
Sinai, 24
Sinai, Mount (*see* Mount Sinai)
statue
　　of an athlete, 74
　　of Claudius, 8
　　of Hercules, 20
　　of Moses (by Michelangelo), 22
　　of Nero, 8
sword, 29
synagogue at Capernaum, 4

tabernacle
    artistic reconstruction of, 56
    model of, 51, 52
    model of altar of burnt offering, 45
    model of sacrificial scene, 59
    model of the Ark of the Covenant, 51, 55,
      64
    model of the Most Holy Place, 64
table of showbread (model), 53
temple, Jerusalem, foundation stones of, 15

Tiber River, 2–3

Trajan's Column, 110

vines, 105

weapons, 29

wilderness, Sinai, 24

ABBREVIATIONS

1. Books of the Bible and Apocrypha

1 Chron.	1 Chronicles
2 Chron.	2 Chronicles
1 Cor.	1 Corinthians
2 Cor.	2 Corinthians
1 Esd.	1 Esdras
2 Esd.	2 Esdras
1 John	1 John
2 John	2 John
3 John	3 John
1 Kings	1 Kings
2 Kings	2 Kings
1 Macc.	1 Maccabees
2 Macc.	2 Maccabees
1 Peter	1 Peter
2 Peter	2 Peter
1 Sam.	1 Samuel
2 Sam.	2 Samuel
1 Thess.	1 Thessalonians
2 Thess.	2 Thessalonians
1 Tim.	1 Timothy
2 Tim.	2 Timothy
Acts	Acts
Amos	Amos
Bar.	Baruch
Bel	Bel and the Dragon
Col.	Colossians
Dan.	Daniel
Deut.	Deuteronomy
Eccl.	Ecclesiastes
Ep. Jer.	Epistle of Jeremiah
Eph.	Ephesians
Est.	Esther
Ezek.	Ezekiel
Ex.	Exodus
Ezra	Ezra
Gal.	Galatians
Gen.	Genesis
Hab.	Habakkuk
Hag.	Haggai
Heb.	Hebrews
Hos.	Hosea
Isa.	Isaiah
James	James
Jer.	Jeremiah
Job	Job
Joel	Joel
John	John
Jonah	Jonah
Josh.	Joshua
Jude	Jude
Judg.	Judges
Judith	Judith
Lam.	Lamentations
Lev.	Leviticus
Luke	Luke
Mal.	Malachi
Mark	Mark
Matt.	Matthew
Mic.	Micah
Nah.	Nahum
Neh.	Nehemiah
Num.	Numbers
Obad.	Obadiah
Phil.	Philippians
Philem.	Philemon
Pr. Man.	Prayer of Manassah
Prov.	Proverbs
Ps.	Psalm
Rest. of Est.	The Rest of Esther
Rev.	Revelation
Rom.	Romans
Ruth	Ruth
S. of III Ch.	The Song of the Three Holy Children
Sir.	Sirach/Ecclesiasticus
Song	Song of Songs
Sus.	Susanna
Titus	Titus
Tobit	Tobit
Wisd. Sol.	The Wisdom of Solomon
Zech.	Zechariah
Zeph.	Zephaniah

2. Old and New Testament Pseudepigrapha and Rabbinic Literature

Individual tractates of rabbinic literature follow the abbreviations of the *SBL Handbook of Style*, pp. 79–80. Qumran documents follow standard Dead Sea Scroll conventions.

2 Bar.	*2 Baruch*
3 Bar.	*3 Baruch*
4 Bar.	*4 Baruch*
1 En.	*1 Enoch*
2 En.	*2 Enoch*
3 En.	*3 Enoch*

4 Ezra	4 Ezra
3 Macc.	3 Maccabees
4 Macc.	4 Maccabees
5 Macc.	5 Maccabees
Acts Phil.	Acts of Philip
Acts Pet.	Acts of Peter and the 12 Apostles
Apoc. Elijah	Apocalypse of Elijah
As. Mos.	Assumption of Moses
b.	Babylonian Talmud (+ tractate)
Gos. Thom.	Gospel of Thomas
Jos. Asen.	Joseph and Aseneth
Jub.	Jubilees
Let. Aris.	Letter of Aristeas
m.	Mishnah (+ tractate)
Mek.	Mekilta
Midr.	Midrash I (+ biblical book)
Odes Sol.	Odes of Solomon
Pesiq. Rab.	Pesiqta Rabbati
Pirqe R. El.	Pirqe Rabbi Eliezer
Pss. Sol.	Psalms of Solomon
Rab.	Rabbah (+biblical book); (e.g., Gen. Rab.=Genesis Rabbah)
S. ʿOlam Rab.	Seder ʿOlam Rabbah
Sem.	Semahot
Sib. Or.	Sibylline Oracles
T. Ab.	Testament of Abraham
T. Adam	Testament of Adam
T. Ash.	Testament of Asher
T. Benj.	Testament of Benjamin
T. Dan	Testament of Dan
T. Gad	Testament of Gad
T. Hez.	Testament of Hezekiah
T. Isaac	Testament of Isaac
T. Iss.	Testament of Issachar
T. Jac.	Testament of Jacob
T. Job	Testament of Job
T. Jos.	Testament of Joseph
T. Jud.	Testament of Judah
T. Levi	Testament of Levi
T. Mos.	Testament of Moses
T. Naph.	Testament of Naphtali
T. Reu.	Testament of Reuben
T. Sim.	Testament of Simeon
T. Sol.	Testament of Solomon
T. Zeb.	Testament of Zebulum
Tanh.	Tanhuma
Tg. Isa.	Targum of Isaiah
Tg. Lam.	Targum of Lamentations
Tg. Neof.	Targum Neofiti
Tg. Onq.	Targum Onqelos
Tg. Ps.-J	Targum Pseudo-Jonathan
y.	Jerusalem Talmud (+ tractate)

3. Classical Historians

For an extended list of classical historians and church fathers, see *SBL Handbook of Style*, pp. 84–87. For many works of classical antiquity, the abbreviations have been subjected to the author's discretion; the names of these works should be obvious upon consulting entries of the classical writers in classical dictionaries or encyclopedias.

Eusebius

Eccl. Hist.	Ecclesiastical History

Josephus

Ag. Ap.	Against Apion
Ant.	Jewish Antiquities
J.W.	Jewish War
Life	The Life

Philo

Abraham	On the Life of Abraham
Agriculture	On Agriculture
Alleg. Interp	Allegorical Interpretation
Animals	Whether Animals Have Reason
Cherubim	On the Cherubim
Confusion	On the Confusion of Thomas
Contempl. Life	On the Contemplative Life
Creation	On the Creation of the World
Curses	On Curses
Decalogue	On the Decalogue
Dreams	On Dreams
Drunkenness	On Drunkenness
Embassy	On the Embassy to Gaius
Eternity	On the Eternity of the World
Flaccus	Against Flaccus
Flight	On Flight and Finding
Giants	On Giants
God	On God
Heir	Who Is the Heir?
Hypothetica	Hypothetica
Joseph	On the Life of Joseph
Migration	On the Migration of Abraham
Moses	On the Life of Moses
Names	On the Change of Names
Person	That Every Good Person Is Free
Planting	On Planting
Posterity	On the Posterity of Cain
Prelim. Studies	On the Preliminary Studies
Providence	On Providence
QE	Questions and Answers on Exodus
QG	Questions and Answers on Genesis
Rewards	On Rewards and Punishments
Sacrifices	On the Sacrifices of Cain and Abel
Sobriety	On Sobriety

Spec. Laws	On the Special Laws
Unchangeable	That God Is Unchangeable
Virtues	On the Virtues
Worse	That the Worse Attacks the Better

Apostolic Fathers

1 Clem.	First Letter of Clement
Barn.	Epistle of Barnabas
Clem. Hom.	Ancient Homily of Clement (also called 2 Clement)
Did.	Didache
Herm. Vis.; Sim.	Shepherd of Hermas, Visions; Similitudes
Ignatius	Epistles of Ignatius (followed by the letter's name)
Mart. Pol.	Martyrdom of Polycarp

4. Modern Abbreviations

AASOR	Annual of the American Schools of Oriental Research
AB	Anchor Bible
ABD	Anchor Bible Dictionary
ABRL	Anchor Bible Reference Library
AGJU	Arbeiten zur Geschichte des antiken Judentums und des Urchristentums
AH	Agricultural History
ALGHJ	Arbeiten zur Literatur und Geschichte des Hellenistischen Judentums
AnBib	Analecta biblica
ANRW	Aufstieg und Niedergang der römischen Welt
ANTC	Abingdon New Testament Commentaries
BAGD	Bauer, W., W. F. Arndt, F. W. Gingrich, and F. W. Danker. Greek-English Lexicon of the New Testament and Other Early Christina Literature (2d. ed.)
BA	Biblical Archaeologist
BAFCS	Book of Acts in Its First Century Setting
BAR	Biblical Archaeology Review
BASOR	Bulletin of the American Schools of Oriental Research
BBC	Bible Background Commentary
BBR	Bulletin for Biblical Research
BDB	Brown, F., S. R. Driver, and C. A. Briggs. A Hebrew and English Lexicon of the Old Testament
BDF	Blass, F., A. Debrunner, and R. W. Funk. A Greek Grammar of the New Testament and Other Early Christian Literature
BECNT	Baker Exegetical Commentary on the New Testament
BI	Biblical Illustrator
Bib	Biblica
BibSac	Bibliotheca Sacra
BLT	Brethren Life and Thought
BNTC	Black's New Testament Commentary
BRev	Bible Review
BSHJ	Baltimore Studies in the History of Judaism
BST	The Bible Speaks Today
BSV	Biblical Social Values
BT	The Bible Translator
BTB	Biblical Theology Bulletin
BZ	Biblische Zeitschrift
CBQ	Catholic Biblical Quarterly
CBTJ	Calvary Baptist Theological Journal
CGTC	Cambridge Greek Testament Commentary
CH	Church History
CIL	Corpus inscriptionum latinarum
CPJ	Corpus papyrorum judaicorum
CRINT	Compendia rerum iudaicarum ad Novum Testamentum
CTJ	Calvin Theological Journal
CTM	Concordia Theological Monthly
CTT	Contours of Christian Theology
DBI	Dictionary of Biblical Imagery
DCM	Dictionary of Classical Mythology.
DDD	Dictionary of Deities and Demons in the Bible
DJBP	Dictionary of Judaism in the Biblical Period
DJG	Dictionary of Jesus and the Gospels
DLNT	Dictionary of the Later New Testament and Its Developments
DNTB	Dictionary of New Testament Background
DPL	Dictionary of Paul and His Letters
EBC	Expositor's Bible Commentary
EDBT	Evangelical Dictionary of Biblical Theology
EDNT	Exegetical Dictionary of the New Testament
EJR	Encyclopedia of the Jewish Religion
EPRO	Études préliminaires aux religions orientales dans l'empire romain
EvQ	Evangelical Quarterly
ExpTim	Expository Times
FRLANT	Forschungen zur Religion und Literatur des Alten und Neuen Testament
GNC	Good News Commentary
GNS	Good News Studies

HCNT	*Hellenistic Commentary to the New Testament*
HDB	*Hastings Dictionary of the Bible*
HJP	*History of the Jewish People in the Age of Jesus Christ,* by E. Schürer
HTR	*Harvard Theological Review*
HTS	Harvard Theological Studies
HUCA	*Hebrew Union College Annual*
IBD	*Illustrated Bible Dictionary*
IBS	*Irish Biblical Studies*
ICC	International Critical Commentary
IDB	*The Interpreter's Dictionary of the Bible*
IEJ	*Israel Exploration Journal*
IG	*Inscriptiones graecae*
IGRR	*Inscriptiones graecae ad res romanas pertinentes*
ILS	*Inscriptiones Latinae Selectae*
Imm	*Immanuel*
ISBE	*International Standard Bible Encyclopedia*
Int	*Interpretation*
IvE	*Inschriften von Ephesos*
IVPNTC	InterVarsity Press New Testament Commentary
JAC	*Jahrbuch fur Antike und Christentum*
JBL	*Journal of Biblical Literature*
JETS	*Journal of the Evangelical Theological Society*
JHS	*Journal of Hellenic Studies*
JJS	*Journal of Jewish Studies*
JOAIW	*Jahreshefte des Osterreeichischen Archaologischen Instites in Wien*
JSJ	*Journal for the Study of Judaism in the Persian, Hellenistic, and Roman Periods*
JRS	*Journal of Roman Studies*
JSNT	*Journal for the Study of the New Testament*
JSNTSup	Journal for the Study of the New Testament: Supplement Series
JSOT	*Journal for the Study of the Old Testament*
JSOTSup	Journal for the Study of the Old Testament: Supplement Series
JTS	*Journal of Theological Studies*
KTR	*Kings Theological Review*
LCL	Loeb Classical Library
LEC	Library of Early Christianity
LSJ	Liddell, H. G., R. Scott, H. S. Jones. *A Greek-English Lexicon*
MM	Moulton, J. H., and G. Milligan. *The Vocabulary of the Greek Testament*
MNTC	Moffatt New Testament Commentary
NBD	*New Bible Dictionary*
NC	Narrative Commentaries
NCBC	New Century Bible Commentary Eerdmans
NEAE	*New Encyclopedia of Archaeological Excavations in the Holy Land*
NEASB	*Near East Archaeological Society Bulletin*
New Docs	*New Documents Illustrating Early Christianity*
NIBC	New International Biblical Commentary
NICNT	New International Commentary on the New Testament
NIDNTT	*New International Dictionary of New Testament Theology*
NIGTC	New International Greek Testament Commentary
NIVAC	NIV Application Commentary
NorTT	*Norsk Teologisk Tidsskrift*
NoT	*Notes on Translation*
NovT	*Novum Testamentum*
NovTSup	Novum Testamentum Supplements
NTAbh	Neutestamentliche Abhandlungen
NTS	*New Testament Studies*
NTT	New Testament Theology
NTTS	New Testament Tools and Studies
OAG	*Oxford Archaeological Guides*
OCCC	*Oxford Companion to Classical Civilization*
OCD	*Oxford Classical Dictionary*
ODCC	*The Oxford Dictionary of the Christian Church*
OGIS	*Orientis graeci inscriptiones selectae*
OHCW	*The Oxford History of the Classical World*
OHRW	*Oxford History of the Roman World*
OTP	*Old Testament Pseudepigrapha,* ed. by J. H. Charlesworth
PEQ	*Palestine Exploration Quarterly*
PG	*Patrologia graeca*
PGM	*Papyri graecae magicae: Die griechischen Zauberpapyri*
PL	*Patrologia latina*
PNTC	Pelican New Testament Commentaries
Rb	*Revista biblica*
RB	*Revue biblique*
RivB	*Rivista biblica italiana*
RTR	*Reformed Theological Review*
SB	Sources bibliques
SBL	Society of Biblical Literature

SBLDS	Society of Biblical Literature Dissertation Series
SBLMS	Society of Biblical Literature Monograph Series
SBLSP	*Society of Biblical Literature Seminar Papers*
SBS	Stuttgarter Bibelstudien
SBT	Studies in Biblical Theology
SCJ	*Stone-Campbell Journal*
Scr	*Scripture*
SE	*Studia Evangelica*
SEG	*Supplementum epigraphicum graecum*
SJLA	Studies in Judaism in Late Antiquity
SJT	*Scottish Journal of Theology*
SNTSMS	Society for New Testament Studies Monograph Series
SSC	Social Science Commentary
SSCSSG	Social-Science Commentary on the Synoptic Gospels
Str-B	Strack, H. L., and P. Billerbeck. *Kommentar zum Neuen Testament aus Talmud und Midrasch*
TC	Thornapple Commentaries
TDNT	*Theological Dictionary of the New Testament*
TDOT	*Theological Dictionary of the Old Testament*
TLNT	*Theological Lexicon of the New Testament*
TLZ	*Theologische Literaturzeitung*
TNTC	Tyndale New Testament Commentary
TrinJ	*Trinity Journal*
TS	*Theological Studies*
TSAJ	Texte und Studien zum antiken Judentum
TWNT	*Theologische Wörterbuch zum Neuen Testament*
TynBul	*Tyndale Bulletin*
WBC	Word Biblical Commentary Waco: Word, 1982

WMANT	Wissenschaftliche Monographien zum Alten und Neuen Testament
WUNT	Wissenschaftliche Untersuchungen zum Neuen Testament
YJS	Yale Judaica Series
ZNW	*Zeitschrift fur die neutestamentliche Wissenschaft und die Junde der alteren Kirche*
ZPE	*Zeischrift der Papyrolgie und Epigraphkik*
ZPEB	*Zondervan Pictorial Encyclopedia of the Bible*

5. General Abbreviations

ad. loc.	in the place cited
b.	born
c., ca.	circa
cf.	compare
d.	died
ed(s).	editors(s), edited by
e.g.	for example
ET	English translation
frg.	fragment
i.e.	that is
ibid.	in the same place
idem	the same (author)
lit.	literally
l(1)	line(s)
MSS	manuscripts
n.d.	no date
NS	New Series
par.	parallel
passim	here and there
repr.	reprint
ser.	series
s.v.	*sub verbo*, under the word
trans.	translator, translated by; transitive

Zondervan Illustrated Bible Backgrounds Commentary

HEBREWS

by George H. Guthrie

Who Wrote Hebrews?

Unlike most other New Testament works, the book of Hebrews does not reveal the identity of its author. Since the second century, people have loved to speculate concerning that identity. The early church fathers were mixed in their opinion on the matter. Scholars of the eastern part of the Mediterranean world often suggested that the apostle Paul wrote the book. Scholars in the West, focused in Rome, argued against that opinion. Even those who held to Pauline authorship, such as Clement of Alexandria and Origen, recognized that the style of the book differs sharply from Paul's writings.

ROME

The Tiber River.
◀

▶ Hebrews
IMPORTANT FACTS:

- **AUTHOR:** Unknown, but someone like Apollos.
- **DATE:** Approximately A.D. 64–66.
- **OCCASION:**
  - To address the problem of apostasy among the recipients.
  - To bolster the resolve of Christians facing persecution.
  - To challenge the believers to move on to maturity, in terms of theological understanding and practical obedience.
  - To address friction between the members of the church and their leaders.
- **THEMES:**
  1. God has spoken and we should obey him.
  2. God has spoken ultimately in the person and work of his Son.
  3. The Son is incarnate and exalted.
  4. The high-priestly ministry of the Son is manifested through his death and exaltation.
  5. The Son's person and work form a superior basis for perseverance in the face of trial.
  6. There are terrible consequences for those who reject the salvation provided by the Son's person and work.

Today few scholars of any theological tradition hold to Pauline authorship for the following reasons. (1) Many of the book's images, theological motifs, and terms are not found in the Pauline literature. For instance, the image of Christ as high priest is unique to Hebrews, and 169 words used in Hebrews are not used anywhere else in the New Testament. (2) The author introduces his quotations of the Old Testament in a different manner from what Paul normally does. Paul usually uses the phrase, "It is written"; Hebrews, following the style of sermons in the Greek-speaking, Jewish synagogues of the Mediterranean world, introduces scriptural quotations with some form of God speaking (e.g., "he says"). (3) Finally, the author of Hebrews depicts himself as having received the gospel from the original witnesses commissioned by the Lord (2:3), and, in light of his often-made assertions to the contrary, it is difficult to imagine Paul making such a statement![1]

Through the centuries other names have been put forward, such as Luke, Clement of Rome, Barnabas, Jude, Apollos, Philip, Silvanus, and Priscilla. What do we know about the author who wrote this intriguing book?

First, the author is a dynamic preacher who really knows his Old Testament and has been trained in the forms of interpretation common in Jewish synagogues. The synagogue was the center of social and religious life for the Jews, and the worship service was at the center of the synagogue service. Focal to the worship service was an exposition of what we now call the Old Testament Scriptures. Hebrews exhibits a number of characteristics of a first-century sermon. The author uses techniques and patterns in his expositions of the Old Testament that were common sermonic features, and he uses these techniques and patterns with great skill and eloquence. Moreover, the book is packed with references to the Old Testament. There are some thirty-

THE SYNAGOGUE AT CAPERNAUM

(left) Aerial view of the remains.

(right) The lintel above the entrance.

▼

five quotations, thirty-four allusions, and numerous summaries of material and references to names and topics given. What is clear is that the author has a broad grasp of Scripture and a heart committed to its authority.

Second, the person who wrote Hebrews is obviously highly educated, which means that he has advanced training in rhetoric. At the heart of ancient rhetorical training was education in the art of expression and argumentation, and numerous stylistic forms were learned as tools to these ends. Such forms are found throughout Hebrews, so the author brings a wealth of education to bear on his task of communicating his message.

Third, the author serves as a Christian leader of the church and exhibits a deep concern for the spiritual state of the book's recipients. All of his background in the synagogue forms of preaching, his copious understanding of the Old Testament, and his training in the art of rhetoric are brought to bear on the task of challenging this group of Christians to stay the course of commitment to Christ. He shows a detailed understanding of the congregation's past and present situations and demonstrates great urgency about their condition.

Although any suggestion as to the authorship of Hebrews must remain in the category of a "best guess," a number of scholars since the time of Martin Luther have followed the Reformer in putting forth Apollos as the best guess on who penned the work. In Acts 18:24–26 Luke describes Apollos as follows:

Meanwhile a Jew named Apollos, a native of Alexandria, came to Ephesus. He was a learned man, with a thorough knowledge of the Scriptures. He had been instructed in the way of the Lord, and he spoke with great fervor and

taught about Jesus accurately, though he knew only the baptism of John. He began to speak boldly in the synagogue.

Several of the descriptors used by Luke of this early Christian leader seem to fit the author of Hebrews. (1) Apollos was from Alexandria, and numerous terms used in Hebrews are also found in the works of Philo of Alexandria and Wisdom of Solomon, a book also associated with that city. We should not overstate the significance of the verbal parallels here since these literary achievements enjoyed wide readership in the Mediterranean world, but the vocabulary shared by these works from Alexandria and Hebrews does provide a possible connection with Apollos. (2) Luke refers to Apollos as "a learned man." The Greek term can also be translated as "eloquent" and was used of those with rhetorical

ITALY
▼

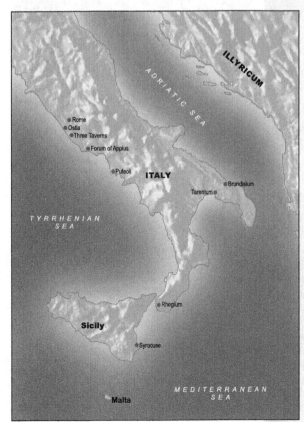

training. Alexandria was a major center for such training. (3) Luke writes that Apollos had a thorough grasp of the Scriptures (i.e., the Old Testament) and spoke with great fervor in the synagogue. Hebrews demonstrates a broad understanding of the Old Testament and a great fervor, and it exhibits characteristics of a synagogue homily in Greek-speaking synagogues of that time. While with Origen we must confess that only God knows who wrote Hebrews, we can also reasonably say that "someone like Apollos" wrote the book.[2]

▶

ROME

(right) The Arch of Constantine.

(bottom) The Via Sacra leading to the Colosseum.

▼

To Whom Was Hebrews Written and Why?

The Recipients. As is the case with authorship, the first recipients of Hebrews are not explicitly identified in the book. What the interpreter is left to, therefore, is sorting through clues to their identity. Fortunately, a number of such clues exist.

First, the author seems to address a group of people who have some background in the Jewish synagogue. His use of the Old Testament seems to assume a fairly broad understanding of the Scriptures. Also, theological concepts popular in the Greek-speaking synagogues of the day are found in the book—such as a special veneration of Moses, the mediatorial role of angels in relation to the old covenant law, and interest in the role of the divine Wisdom in creation.

Second, some associated with this Christian community seem to have abandoned the Christian faith and, perhaps, returned to Judaism proper, and others are struggling with the temptation to do so.

Third, the church addressed is likely located in the city of Rome. Among the over one million inhabitants of Rome in the first Christian century, some forty to sixty thousand were Jews. Many of these were Roman citizens, had Greek or Latin names, and spoke Greek. Acts 2 tells us that there were Jews from Rome at the Pentecost event, and it may be that some of these converted to Christianity, returning to the capital to establish a church there. In Hebrews 13:24 the author writes, "Those from Italy send you their greetings." Although the phrase "from Italy" is ambiguous, the same phrase is used of Aquila and Priscilla in Acts 18:2. In context it refers to those from Rome who then reside somewhere other than

Rome. Therefore, it seems that the author is writing back to Rome while associated with some who are from there.

A second point in favor of a Roman destination is that the earliest documented use of Hebrews in the early church is in a pastoral letter known as *First Clement*, a letter written by Clement of Rome to the church at Corinth. Hebrews' influence is seen throughout the work.

Finally, only Hebrews among the New Testament documents refers to those who govern the church as "leaders" (*hegoumenoi*, a participle used as a noun), although Acts 15:22 (RSV) uses the same Greek term adjectively to describe the delegation, "leading men," sent to Antioch with the decision of the Jerusalem council. This designation for church leadership is also found in the books of *First Clement* and *The Shepherd of Hermas*, both of which are associated with the church in Rome.

Therefore, in all likelihood the first recipients of Hebrews are a Jewish Christian community in the city of Rome that has members struggling with enduring in their Christian commitment.

What Was the Author Attempting to Accomplish?

Consequently, the author of the book has a specific goal in view—to encourage those who are faltering spiritually to endure in the faith. He attempts to accomplish this goal by an interworking of theology and exhortation. In fact, the book is structured around a movement back and forth between teachings about Jesus as Son of God and great high priest, and strong exhortations to be faithful to him.[3] The main expositional sections about Christ deal with his superiority to the angels (1:5–14), the necessity of his incarnation (2:10–18), his appointment as superior high priest (5:1–10; 7:1–28), and the superiority of his heavenly offering for sins (8:3–10:18). Woven throughout the rest of the book are exhortation sections made up of positive and negative examples, warnings and promises, general encouragement and expressions of deep concern. These two great streams of theology and exhortation are masterfully woven together to communicate a central message: *Jesus provides a superior basis for relating to God and enduring in that relationship, and those who reject him are in deep trouble!*

When Was Hebrews Written?

If we have assessed rightly the destination of Hebrews as the city of Rome, several facts gleaned from the book help to narrow the date of writing. The recipients have been Christians for a while (5:11–6:3) and at some time in the past have faced rather severe persecution for the faith (10:32–34). Yet, it seems that although they are facing an increasing intensity of persecution at present, at the time of writing they have yet to face martyrdom (12:4). These facts point to sometime in the mid–60s A.D., just before an escalating and severe time of persecution instigated by Emperor Nero. In the mid–60s the church had existed for some three decades. In A.D. 49 the

NERO

A coin depicting the emperor (A.D. 54–68).

Christian community seems to have had harsh conflicts with the Jewish community, resulting in a general expulsion of all Jews by the emperor Claudius. This could be the persecution referred to in 10:32–34. Also, the rise of Nero's terrible persecution of Christians in Rome in the mid–60s would account for the faltering of some in the church.

How Is Hebrews Relevant for Today?

The Gospels and Paul's letters have overshadowed the study and teaching of Hebrews for a number of reasons, not the least of which is the complexity of the book. However, Hebrews is a rich mine of theological insight and pastoral encouragement, and it has much to say to the modern-day church. Foremost of all, Hebrews speaks to the challenge of perseverance in the Christian life over

against "falling away" from God. In a day in which thousands every year abandon the church, either in overt rejection or quiet separation, the church needs to address the problem and what to do about it. Thousands more worldwide are caught in the crucible of persecution and put under pressure to leave the faith. In relation to these matters, Hebrews demonstrates the foundational nature of theology for Christian life and practice.

The author uses his extensive exposition on the Son of God as the *basis* for his exhortation material in the book. Right thinking, Hebrews suggests, leads to right choices in life. Thus, this Jewish-Christian sermon champions a clear view of Christ and his superiority to other ways of approaching God as mandatory for perseverance in true Christianity. Further, the book challenges Christians to choose a path of drawing near to God and to the Christian community as the

▶

ROMAN EMPERORS

(left) Nero (A.D. 54–68).

(right) Claudius (A.D. 41–54)

◀

**ROMAN
COLOSSEUM**

The photo shows
the interior of the
structure and the
labyrinth beneath
the stadium floor.

relational bases of endurance. Christianity at heart is a relational religion, and Hebrews presents a clear picture of community as vital for correct living. Therefore, once the modern reader begins to sort through the twists and turns of Hebrews' argument and the background of its thought world, a rich depository of encouragement and spiritual nourishment is tapped. If, as a Christian community, we can see Jesus more clearly (3:1; 12:1–2), draw near to God more consistently (4:14–16; 10:19–23), and encourage one another more readily (3:13; 10:24–25), Hebrews will have served us well.

Introduction (1:1–4)

As noted above, it is a widely held opinion that Hebrews constitutes a first-century sermon rather than a letter. In both the contexts of the Jewish synagogue and the forums in which speeches were delivered in the broader Greco-Roman culture, much emphasis was placed on an address beginning with a powerful and appropriate introduction, also referred to as a *proem* or *exordium*. Jewish sermons often started with a reference to the text to be expounded. Greek rhetoricians saw the introduction as well-crafted if it accomplished two goals. (1) The introduction should sum up the primary topic or topics to be discussed in the speech. Aristotle, whose work on rhetoric was used in rhetorical training in the first century, likened the introduction to a prelude in a performance on the flute because it paves the way for what follows.[4] (2) The word-crafters of the day suggested that an introduction should capture the attention of the audience rather than allow the hearers to drift into disinterest. Philo of Alexandria, a contemporary of the author of Hebrews, writes concerning Moses' introduction to the book of Genesis: "His exordium . . . is one that excites our admiration in the highest degree."[5] This compliment can also be applied to Hebrews. Here in the introduction to the book the author presents the primary topics that will be detailed in the sermon (e.g., God, God's Word, the Son, the Son's superiority and sacrifice) and does so with flair, using such stylistic devices as parallelism and alliteration (five words in 1:1 begin with the Greek letter *p*).

God spoke (1:1). The concept of "God speaking" must be understood against the backdrop of the author's orientation to what we know as the Old Testament. In the sermons and writings of Greek-speaking synagogues of the Greco-Roman era, Old Testament quotations most often were introduced as being spoken by God. In this tradition Hebrews almost always utilizes forms of the Greek word *legō* ("to say"), with God as the speaker. Thus the author of Hebrews utilizes the Old Testament text extensively as a basis of proclamation and exhortation. One of his main presuppositions is that God has spoken his authoritative word, and people should hear and obey it.

REFLECTIONS

THE NEED TO HEAR GOD'S VOICE through his Word has not changed. You and I need to hear it today both for its encouragement and correction. What avenues are providing you with that opportunity? Are you hearing the Word preached consistently? Do you have habits of Bible reading and reflection? If you are studying, are you also "hearing" in the sense of applying the Word obediently? God has spoken; we should listen.

To our forefathers (1:1). The reference to "forefathers" is a generic designation meaning "ancestors," rather than a specific reference to the patriarchs of the Jewish faith. The term refers to all the people of God to whom the prophets spoke, who are considered by the author to be spiritual ancestors of those addressed by Hebrews (cf. 1 Cor. 10:1, which was written to a primarily Gentile audience).[6] The practice of noting God's relationship with past generations has a rich tradition in the biblical and extra-biblical Jewish literature; it presupposes God's consistency through the centuries in dealing with his people. For example, Tobit 8:5 proclaims in part, "Blessed are you, O God of our ancestors, and blessed is your name in all generations forever."

Through the prophets (1:1). Prophets were known in broader Greek culture—for example, in connection with the oracle of Delphi.[7] Yet, Hebrews' reference here points directly to the prophets of Jewish history. The noun *nambî,* is found 309 times in the Old Testament, 92 of these occurring in the book of Jeremiah. The designation must not be seen as restricted to the so-called "writing prophets," such as Isaiah and Amos, nor even to other bearers of the prophetic mantel such as Samuel and Elijah. In the Old Testament, figures such as Abraham (Gen. 20:7), Moses (Deut. 34:10), Aaron (Ex. 7:1), and Miriam (Ex. 15:20) were called "prophet/prophetess."[8] In Hebrews 1:1 the author probably has in mind all those through whom God delivered divine revelation (cf. David referred to as such in 4:7). That revelation came "at various times," meaning it varied temporally, and "in various ways," referring to the diversity of forms it took. To name a few, God spoke through dreams, visions, mighty acts, appearances, commands, and promises.

In these last days (1:2). Old Testament prophets spoke of a "day" or "days" in which the Lord would judge his enemies and redeem his people.[9] In some New Testament passages the reference to the "last days" is forward-looking, emphasizing the consummation of the ages and the final judgment.[10] Yet, it is clear that both Peter's use of the phrase at Pentecost, attached as it is to the quotation of Joel 2:28 (Acts 2:17), and the use here in Hebrews speak of "the last days" as having been inaugurated in the person and ministry of Christ. These references follow a classic Jewish apocalyptic conception of history as divided into two stages, the former times and the end times. The Qumran community also understood itself as living in the last days of human history.[11] In Hebrews' Christian conception, the "former times" constitute the era prior to the coming of the Christ, and the "last days" the era of Christ's kingdom.

By his Son, whom he appointed heir of all things (1:2). In Greco-Roman cultures the exact laws of inheritance varied from the fifth century B.C. to the second century A.D. Sons were the primary heirs in earlier times, but later on, in certain circumstances, wives, daughters, and mistresses could also be heirs.[12] Nevertheless, the practice of inheritance had great social import throughout the cultures of the Mediterranean, and the concept was undoubtedly an important one to the first hearers of Hebrews. In biblical literature, the land was the Lord's, and as a privilege and blessing he gave it as an inheritance to Israel. Thus the concept of inheritance was tied to possession of the land and the importance of land to a family. Thus in the ancient world an heir was one with authority to utilize or administer some possession.[13]

When having to do with royal families, however, the inheritance often was expansive, involving the transfer of a kingdom. The reference to the Son as "heir" in 1:2 alludes to a royal psalm (Ps. 2:8), which the author of Hebrews also quotes at Hebrews 1:5: "Ask of me, and I will make the nations your inheritance, the ends of the earth your possession." In context, this psalm addresses the rebellion of the nations against God and God's rebuke of them. The content of that rebuke largely has to do with the enthronement of his Son, who will rule the nations with strength and crush any form of insurrection with his "iron scepter." Those nations that are wise, however, will submit themselves to the Anointed One (Ps. 2:11–12) and will find cause for rejoicing. Regardless of the nations' response, however, the extent of the Son's rule comes through clearly as "the ends of the earth." All are subject to his will. The author expands this idea to "all things," meaning the whole created order.

Radiance of God's glory (1:3). In the biblical literature "glory" when used in relation to God speaks of the radiant manifestation of his presence.[14] To see God's glory, therefore, was to witness the presence of God. The term *apaugasma*, rendered here as "radiance," indicates intense brightness or splendor.[15] Philo, commenting on humanity's legacy from Adam, suggests that, in their minds, people are connected to the divine logos, or reason, because they come into being as a "ray" of that "blessed nature."[16] Philo's main point in the context is identification or kinship with Adam, the first father of humanity, in his connection to God as creator. In Wisdom of Solomon 7:26 divine wisdom is praised as follows: "For she is a reflection [*apaugasma*] of eternal light, a spotless mirror of the working of God, and an image of his goodness." Again, close association is the emphasis here. Hebrews' point is related but framed from a Christian point of view. The author wishes to proclaim the close relationship between the Father and the Son. Just as one cannot separate the brightness of light from the light itself, one cannot separate seeing the Son from witnessing the presence of God, since the Son manifests the person of God.[17]

The exact representation of his being (1:3). The word translated "representation" (*charaktēr*), used only here in the New Testament, originally was used for an engraving tool or an engraver, a stamp, or even a branding iron. It also came to be used of the image, impress, or mark made, for example on coins or seals. Metaphorically the word developed the meaning of a distinguishing mark on a person or thing by which it is distinguished from other persons or things.[18] Thus, the term denotes features of an object or person by which one is able to identify it.[19] Philo of Alexandria uses the word fifty-one times in his works, and it is possible that the author of Hebrews has picked up the term in interaction with Philo's works. Yet, as William Lane points out, our author employs the word to make his point for Christian theology.[20] The idea that the Son is the "exact representation of [God's] being" means that he gives a clear picture of the nature of God. This echoes other New Testament texts that speak of Jesus as the "form," "likeness," or "image" of the Father.[21]

Sustaining all things by his powerful word (1:3). In the ancient Orient a word was often conceived of as a powerful force, for instance in the use of blessings or spells. Gods especially were understood to have words of dynamic power that could create, sustain, or destroy. The words of God in the Old Testament have such force, of course. The heavens were made by his dynamic word,[22] and God's voice is heard in the booming of the storm as well as other aspects of nature. God interacts with the world he has made (Ps. 29). More significantly, the creative word of God is tied to the governing word of God in Psalm 33. The God of nature is also the God who works out his plans among the nations and people. This is the sense of the Son "sustaining all things by his powerful word" in Hebrews 1:3. This is not an echo of the mighty Atlas holding the weight of the world on his shoulders. Rather, it speaks of the Son's governmental power to bring all of the created order, including people, to his desired ends. Under the Son's direction history is progressing according to his plan.

He sat down at the right hand (1:3). The imagery of "sitting at the right hand," con-

SEALS

Hebrew seals (*bulae*) dating from the seventh century B.C.

▼

tained in this allusion to Psalm 110:1, has a rich background in the Old Testament as well as pagan and extrabiblical Jewish literature. For instance, Athena is depicted by Pindar of Cynoscephalae as sitting at the right hand of Zeus.[23] In the Canaanite *Poem of Baal* the architect, Koshar, sits at the right hand of Baal as they discuss plans for Baal's temple.[24] Egyptian art often portrays the pharaoh as sitting on a throne to the right of a god.[25] The concept of the "right hand" was primarily used in the Old Testament to represent either superior power, rank, or honor. In Psalm 80:17 a person whom Yahweh uses for the accomplishment of his purposes is described as "at [his] right hand." Bathsheba was given the honor of sitting on Solomon's right hand (1 Kings 2:19), and the right hand position was occupied by the bride at the marriage ceremony of an unnamed monarch (Ps. 45:9). At Yahweh's right hand are an abundance of pleasures (16:11), learning (45:4), and righteousness (48:10). Psalm 110:1 is a royal psalm that speaks of the "Lord" being seated at Yahweh's right hand in a rank of power, as demonstrated by the subjugation of his enemies. The New Testament utilizes this psalm more than any other Old Testament text, heralding its fulfillment in the exaltation of Jesus.[26]

The name (1:4). The word rendered here as "name" (*onoma*) was used variously to mean name, status, rank, fame, or person. A papyrus of the third century A.D., for example, speaks of questionable officials who have devised "offices" (*onomata*) for themselves.[27] Richard Longenecker points out that "the Name," initially used as a pious reference to God, came to be employed among first-century Jewish Christians as a title for Jesus.[28] In Ephesians 1:21 and Philippians 2:9, as well as Hebrews 1:4, Jesus' "name" is above every name. What the Son has inherited, therefore, is a rank or title of power and divinity that formerly was used of God alone.

Angels (1:5). Angels serve many roles in the biblical story, including that of messengers (e.g., Matt. 1:18–25), providers of practical help (e.g., 1 Kings 19:5–7),

> ▶ **A String of Old Testament Passages Bearing Witness to Christ's Superiority (1:5–14)**

Jewish interpreters of the New Testament era, including the rabbis, early Christians, and scholars of the Qumran community, produced what have been called "chain quotations" or "a string of pearls." Such strings of quotations were brought together on the basis of common words and served to support an argument by virtue of the quantity of scriptural evidence brought to bear. The idea was to document so much scriptural material on a given topic that the audience would be persuaded to agree with the scholar's conclusion. Hebrews 1:5–14 contains such a string of quotations, consisting of three pairs of passages proclaiming the superiority of the Son over the angels, followed by a climactic quotation of Psalm 110:1. The first pair (2 Sam. 7:14; Ps. 2:7) asserts the Son's superiority by virtue of his unique relationship with God the Father (Heb. 1:5). The Son's superiority may be seen vis-à-vis the inferior status of the angels through the second pair of Old Testament passages.[A-1] In 1:8–12 the Son's eternal nature and enthronement over the universe provide the focus of the third pair of texts.[A-2] deliverers (Dan. 3; Acts 5:17–24), and guides (Gen. 24:7). They also serve God as those who carry out his wrath (e.g., Ps. 78:49) and sometimes act as interpreters of divine revelation (Rev. 22:6).[29] Their role largely has to do with ministering to people on God's behalf.

For to which of the angels did God ever say (1:5)? Rhetorical questions formed a common feature of sermons in the Greek-speaking synagogues of the first century. The question amounts to an assertion that God has never said anything of the sort to an angel.

You are my Son; today I have become your Father (1:5). Here the author quotes Psalm 2:7. In its original context Psalm 2 addresses the rebellion of the nations against God and his Anointed One (see comments on Heb. 1:2). Such insurrection will be annihilated by the enthroned king's great power. The concept of the Messiah as God's Son seems to have existed in Judaism prior to the advent of Christianity. A manuscript from Qumran (4Q246), says that the Messiah "will be called son of God; they will call him son of the Most High."[30] The early Christians applied Psalm 2 to Jesus, understanding the victory heralded as God's victory over the earthly forces opposed to the church.[31] Specifically, this psalm is understood as God's open proclamation of his relationship with the Son.

I will be his Father, and he will be my Son (1:5). Second Samuel 7:14 presents the words of Nathan the prophet to David, promising him that one of his descendants will have an eternal kingdom. The author of Hebrews understands that promise as fulfilled in the person of Christ. He ties this passage to Psalm 2:7

by virtue of the term "son" that the two passages have in common. Interpreters of the era would interpret one passage in light of another with a common term or phrase, or present two together in an argument. This practice, used extensively throughout Hebrews, is called "verbal analogy."

Firstborn (1:6). In the ancient world the term *prōtotokos* most often referred to the firstborn offspring of either a human or an animal. The concept's background in Jewish history and literature is rich, especially in relation to the consecration of the firstborn to Yahweh.[32] In the Old Testament era a firstborn son had a special place in his father's heart, shared in the authority of the father, and inherited the larger share of his property.[33] In the New Testament the word most often serves as a title for Christ and is an expression of his preeminence in both the church and the cosmos. It is especially used in relation to the resurrection.[34]

He makes his angels winds, his servants flames of fire (1:7). The original context of Psalm 104:4 has to do with God's lordship over nature, and in the Hebrew suggests that the winds are God's messengers and flames of fire his servants. Old Testament scholars point out, however, the strong strand of tradition in the Old Testament in which the natural phenomena of wind and fire are associated with angels.[35] This tradition is picked up in a wide range of Jewish literature, including the targums and literature from Qumran, and is probably why the Septuagint translates the Hebrew text so overtly as a reference to the angels. The point for the author of Hebrews is that the angels are *servants*, serving in a role inferior to that of the Son.

Anointing you with the oil of joy (1:9). Olive oil had a wide variety of uses in the ancient world, including cooking, lighting, skin conditioning, and medical treatments.[36] Significantly for the use of Psalm 45:6–7 in Hebrews 1:8–9, oil also was used to anoint Israelite kings, priests, and prophets upon their installation into their office (e.g., 1 Sam. 10:1; 1 Kings 19:15–16).[37] By his anointing the king was shown to be above his companions. By his exaltation Christ has been enthroned as king of the universe and shown to be superior.

Laid the foundations of the earth (1:10). Cities and buildings of the biblical era were only as structurally stable as their foundations. A bed of rock often was used. Solomon's temple, for example, used large, expensive blocks of stone for the foundation, and the foundations of ancient buildings often are the only remaining part of an ancient building today.[38] The image of a foundation can be used to point out the devastating circumstances of a life not built on God's Word and will over against the stability

of a life grounded in truth, as in Jesus' treatment of the two foundations (Matt. 7:24–27). Yet in Hebrews 1:10 the imagery directs our attention elsewhere. As creator of the cosmos, the Lord has "built" the earth as a master architect. That he laid its "foundations" means he is the one who has given the earth its structural integrity. The earth has endured the test of time because it has been well crafted in the beginning. Hebrews 1:10 praises the Son as the creator of the world.

They will all wear out like a garment. You will roll them up like a robe; like a garment they will be changed (1:11–12). Although some variety in clothing existed throughout the biblical times, people generally wore some type of tunic, normally extending from the shoulders to at least the knees. A cloak was worn over the tunic at times, especially in cooler weather. As perishable items, pieces of clothing wore out over time, as they do today. The imagery used in 1:10–11 is that of taking off and putting away an old article of clothing. Although the earth has been made by the Son and given a sure foundation (1:10), it is not eternal; it will eventually "wear out" like an old article of clothing. By contrast, the Son, who laid its foundation in the beginning, will be there to pack it away in the end. He "is the same" (13:8), the eternal one who is superior by virtue of his eternal nature.

A Warning About Rejecting the Word of Salvation (2:1–4)

One of the key roles of ancient speakers, rhetoricians and rabbis alike, was to motivate people to take specific courses of action, and they utilized a wide variety of

◀ *left*

FOUNDATION

Herodian-era foundation stones in Jerusalem.

oratorical and literary tools to accomplish that end. One such tool was the "argument from lesser to greater," also known as an a fortiori argument. This device lies at the heart of 2:1–4. This type of argument reasoned that if some principle is true in a less important situation, then it certainly is true—and has greater implications—in a more important situation. The author of Hebrews dynamically follows this logic by making first an assertion with which his audience certainly would agree: The law of the old covenant was binding and the breaking of that law had very negative consequences (2:2). This, for the author, is the "lesser" situation. The "greater" situation surrounds the giving of the word of salvation through the Lord Jesus, this message of salvation being confirmed by the apostles and God himself. His reasoning is that if punishment followed rejection of the law, it certainly will follow rejection of the word of salvation.

So that we do not drift away (2:1). The concept of drifting provides a powerful image for the spiritual state against which the audience is warned. The term translated "drift" (*pararyomai*) could be used of something that slipped from

DRIFT AWAY

A column in Rome in honor of the emperor Marcus Aurelius (A.D. 161–180) depicting Roman merchant ships. ▼

REFLECTIONS

THE CULTURE OF THE MODERN, Western world is increasingly uncomfortable with the concept of punishment being attached to religion. Yet the concept constitutes a cornerstone of biblical revelation and relates directly to the problems of sin and human beings' desire for self-legislation. It must be insisted from a biblical worldview that modern opposition to the concept of punishment also fails to deal adequately with the problem of sin. How do you respond to this conflict in worldviews? Do you take the consequences of sin seriously?

one's person, such as a ring that accidentally slipped off a finger. It also could be employed to indicate something or someone heading in the wrong direction. For instance, if someone choked on a piece of food—the morsel going down the windpipe instead of to the stomach—this word could be used to describe the misdirection.[39] A nautical image, however, comes closer to the concept of drifting and may reflect more nearly the author's concern since the word translated "pay . . . attention" in 2:1 was used as a technical term for bringing a ship into port.[40] The wind or oars powered ancient ships. A test of a captain's skill in controlling a large, wind-driven vessel came upon entering a harbor and approaching a dock, since there were no "reverse engines" to slow the ship's progress. To carry too much speed would result in crashing into the docks; to carry too little speed resulted in falling short. A ship in the latter instance would "drift" by the place at which it was supposed to land, perhaps being impeded or driven off course by strong currents or prevailing winds. Thus, the author of Hebrews expresses concern over the spiritual state of his readers, whom he fears may be drifting off course from a clear focus on the gospel of salvation.

The message spoken by angels was binding (2:2). The idea that God gave the law on Sinai through angels was commonly held among Jews of the Greek-speaking synagogues in the first-century Mediterranean world and matches the broader witness of the Old Testament that God often delivered messages through angels. Josephus writes, "And for ourselves, we have learned from God the most excellent of our teachings, and the most holy part of our law by angels."[41] In the New Testament both Acts 7:38 and Galatians 3:19 echo this belief. As pointed out with reference to Hebrews 1:7, angels were often associated with natural elements such as wind and lightning, and it may be that the manifestation of these elements at Sinai came to be associated with angelic beings. Also, Psalm 68:17 notes that the chariots of God were with the Lord at Sinai, which implies for some interpreters that angels were with the Lord on the holy mountain.

The old covenant law was "binding" (*bebaios*), a legal term, in that it was so sure and durable as to be unchanging. In legal contexts of the first century this word and its relatives referred to a legal guarantee.[42] Philo wrote that the law of Moses is "firm" (*bebaios*), unshakable, and unchangeable, being planted firmly so as to endure forever.[43] Thus, a person under that law was obligated legally to follow it or face punishment. For example, punishment was handed out for the sins of murder (Num. 35:16–21), adultery, incest, bestiality, and sodomy.[44] The guilty party received from God in accordance with his sin, and there was no escaping God's judgment.[45]

Which was first announced . . . confirmed . . . God also testified (2:3–4). This message of salvation announced by

---

▶ **Salvation**

In Greco-Roman culture "salvation" connoted deliverance from especially perilous situations such as war, shipwrecks, or desert crossings. Plutarch, for instance, tells of one young woman who was "saved" at sea by a dolphin. The most common usage, however, comes in medical contexts. People are "saved" from severe illness, and both medicines and doctors are referred to as "saviors."[A-3]

Broadly speaking, in biblical literature the word, when used theologically, communicates what God has done, is doing, and will do on behalf of people. In the Old Testament God saves from oppression or disaster, preeminently seen in the Exodus from Egypt (Deut. 26:5–9). In the New Testament one may be saved from spiritual or physical dangers, especially from the wrath of God and the coming day of judgment.[A-4] The message of salvation in the New Testament focuses on the deliverance from the consequences of sin by Christ's work, his "announcement" (Heb. 2:3) of the good news of salvation characterizing his ministry (Matt. 9:35). In Hebrews this word of deliverance is played out in high-priestly imagery with Christ as both high priest and sacrifice.

the Lord has been validated to humanity via impressive means, and the author of Hebrews continues with terminology common to the courts of the first century to drive home its legitimacy. The message was "confirmed" by those who first heard the message. Here we find the verb form of the word translated "binding" in 2:2 (see comments). In a court of law or business deal the term referred to something that was guaranteed or legally authenticated to the point of being beyond question. Thus the first hearers of the Lord's message, rather than offering mere hearsay, "confirmed" the word of salvation's veracity in a way that could be counted on absolutely.

Moreover, "God also testified to it by signs, wonders and various miracles, and gifts of the Holy Spirit." God entered the courtroom of history with miraculous works as a joint witness with the first witnesses. Thus he added his stamp of validation on the preaching of the first Christians. The triple expression "signs, wonders and miracles" was used in early Christianity of God's works among his people that attended the preaching of the gospel.[46]

A Transition From a Discussion of Exaltation to One Concerning Incarnation (2:5–9)

Hebrews 2:5–9, by its use of Psalm 8:4–6, serves to move the focus from the exalted status of Christ above the angels to his incarnation, the Psalm having both elements of exaltation ("crowned with glory and honor") and elements of incarnation ("a little lower than the angels"). The author uses this psalm in proximity to Psalm 110:1 (Heb. 1:13),

center ▶

CROWN

the capstone on his discussion of the Son's exaltation, because both Old Testament passages refer to the act of subjecting someone or something under Christ's "feet." Such use of "verbal analogy" was common among the rabbis, who interpreted one passage in light of another that had the same or similar wording. These two psalms are used together elsewhere in the New Testament at 1 Corinthians 15:25–27 to speak of Christ's authority.

It is not to angels that he has subjected the world to come (2:5). The teachers of ancient Judaism believed that angels had been assigned positions of authority over the nations, an interpretation associated with the Greek form of Deuteronomy 32:8, which suggests the boundaries of the earth were established according to the number of God's angels. In Daniel 10:20–21 and 12:1 angels are referred to as "princes" of Persia and Greece and Michael as the "great prince" over God's people. In his exaltation, however, Christ has been positioned over all principalities and powers (e.g., Eph. 1:20–23), an authoritative rule that will be fully known at the end of the age. Thus, it is to him that "the world to come" (an allusion to the phrase "until I make your enemies a footstool for your feet" in Ps. 110:1/Heb. 1:13) has been subjected.

Crowned him with glory and honor (2:7). A crown in the ancient Mediterranean world symbolized royal authority, and both literature and art, spanning the cultures of that world, witness to its significance. The image of the crown used in Psalm 8 originally referred to the dignity of humanity and the unique role of people in God's creation.

The early Christians, however, in conjunction with Psalm 110:1, adopted this psalm as a witness to the exaltation of Christ and, consequently, emphasized the royal overtones inherent in it. A ruler being crowned for a position of authority was familiar to the first hearers of Hebrews. For example, the coinage they used as citizens of the Roman empire often carried the image of the Caesar with a crown on his head. Coins from the reign of Nero, who probably ruled at the time of Hebrews' writing, show him wearing radiant crowns, identifying him with gods such as Apollo and Hercules.[47]

We do not see everything subject to him (2:8). Psalms 8 and 110 each witness to the exaltation of Christ, but the reader notices that the *timing* of subjugation of things or people to Christ is different in these two texts. Psalm 110:1 puts the subjection of Christ's enemies in the future ("until"), and Psalm 8 states the subjection of all things as an accom-

plished fact ("and put everything under his feet"). The author of Hebrews addresses the potential confusion posed by the two passages in fine rabbinic style. The rabbis often sought to dispel confusion and to clarify a point of interpretation when two such texts presented a seeming contradiction. The writer of Hebrews suggests, in light of Psalm 8, that all things have indeed been placed under the feet of Christ (2:8). What Psalm 110:1 means, according to the author, is that we do not yet see all things subject to him at present (2:8–9). Thus, the subjugation of all things to Christ is an accomplished fact that has yet to be consummated. The enemies have been defeated, but the total realization of that victory will be seen in the future. This explanation would have been especially meaningful to the readers of Hebrews, who were facing persecution at the hands of an evil government.

The Purpose of the Incarnation (2:10–18)

Author of their salvation perfect (2:10). The term rendered "author" had a range of meanings as used by ancient authors, including founder (of a family, city, people, nation, or even creation or humanity as a whole), hero or heroine, prince, chief, captain, leader, or scout. Several of these meanings are possible in the given context. Jesus certainly is the founder or originator of salvation, but also can be considered the leader or trailblazer, since he paves the way to glory. Another possibility is hero or champion in this context, since Jesus wins freedom for those who have been held in bondage (2:14–15). For instance, Hercules is often called champion (*archēgos*) and savior in inscriptions, coins, and literature.[48]

REFLECTIONS

IT CAN BE DISCOURAGING WHEN we face trials that appear to be outside of God's concern or control. Prayers for healing or deliverance may seem to get no higher than the ceiling. Yet we must base our beliefs and confidence on what God has shown us to be true through the Scriptures—he alone has perfect perspective on all the dynamics surrounding our present circumstances. Thus, we should remember Jesus, who also suffered when he was here on earth, and look to him as our exalted Lord, who will put things right in his own timing.

Being "perfect" does not mean without flaw—although that certainly is true of Jesus (4:15); rather, it has to do with bringing to completion or being fully equipped. Especially relevant for 2:10 is the use in the LXX of both the noun and verb forms of the term translated "perfection" when referring to the preparation of the Levitical priests for service.[49] Therefore, the word rendered "author" in Hebrews 2:10 may best be understood as having to do with Jesus being the founder or originator of the new covenant religion, since this idea provides a fitting complement to the concept of his being perfected for his high-priestly ministry. Jesus is the founder of our salvation because he has been fully prepared, through suffering on the cross, to serve as our high priest.

▶

HERCULES

A Roman-era bronze statue of the god.

I will declare your name (2:12). The writer to the Hebrews utilizes two Old Testament texts to support the theme of Christ's solidarity with believers—Psalm 22 and Isaiah 8. Sensitivity to the context of each is vital for an understanding of why the passages are used at this point in the book.

The early church received Psalm 22 as a profound prophecy concerning the sufferings of Christ. Psalm 22:1 is the origin of the Son's words of anguish on the cross, "My God, my God, why have you forsaken me?" (Matt. 27:46). Verses 7–8 of the same psalm constitute a taunt by wicked people against the righteous sufferer: "He trusts in God. Let God rescue him," words that echo taunts around the cross (Matt. 27:43). Psalm 22:16–18 tell of the piercing of the sufferer's hands and feet, the wholeness of his bones, and the game played for his clothing.[50] Thus Psalm 22 foreshadows the crucifixion and depicts the excruciating suffering of a righteous person. With Psalm 22:22 (the passage quoted at Heb. 2:12) one finds a shift in mood. Here the righteous one praises God for his help. The psalm supports the author's discussion of the solidarity between Jesus and believers with its reference to "brothers" (i.e., Christians are a part of the Son's family) and the phrase "in the presence of the congregation," which for the author alludes to the incarnation. Thus Psalm 22:22, when understood in light of its Old Testament backdrop, encapsulates a rich statement of Jesus' humanity, suffering, and solidarity with believers.

I will put my trust in him (2:13). Isaiah 8:17–18 also has strong messianic overtones. In 8:14, three verses earlier, the prophet refers to "a stone that causes men to stumble and a rock that makes them fall," words that New Testament authors appropriate as referring to the Messiah (Rom. 9:33; 1 Peter 2:8). The first part of the Isaiah passage quoted in Hebrews states, "I will put my trust in him." Originally this expression of faith stated the prophet's trust in God in the face of the Assyrian crisis. Hebrews applies it to Jesus' trust in the Father. The next phrase, "Here am I, and the children God has given me," points both to the Son's location as among people and his being in a familial relationship with God's children.

The devil (2:14). The Old Testament (e.g., Gen. 3:1–7), and Jewish traditions generally, associate the devil with death. For example, Wisdom of Solomon 2:24 states, "but through the devil's envy death entered the world, and those who belong to his company experience it" (NRSV). Yet, the New Testament is clear that Christ's work has destroyed the devil and his work (1 John 3:8).

Held in slavery by their fear of death (2:15). Specifically, Christ's provision of the forgiveness of sins through his death on the cross has freed those who were slaves to the fear of death. Greco-Roman authors such as Euripides, Cicero,

Seneca, and Epictetus speak of the powerful effect the fear of death has on people. Epictetus states, "And where can I go to escape death? Show me the country, show me the people to whom I may go, upon whom death does not come; show me a magic charm against it. If I have none, what do you wish me to do? I cannot avoid death."[51]

Lucretius, a contemporary of Cicero, wrote a long didactic poem entitled *On The Nature of Things* (*De Rerum Natura*) from an Epicurean perspective. The Epicureans taught that all of reality is material, thus denying an afterlife. Lucretius sought to free people from the fear of death by proclaiming that people cease to exist after death and need not worry about eternal punishment (1.102–26). Thus, the fear of death was associated with the ideas of judgment and consequent punishment both in the Greek and Roman writings.

Although holding a different worldview, Philo, a Jewish writer of the first century, echoes the sentiment, "Nothing is so calculated to enslave the mind as fearing death through desire to live" (*Good Person* 22). Christ, however, by his death that destroyed the work of the devil, has delivered those of the new covenant from such paralyzing fear. His death provides forgiveness of sins and removes the threat of punishment.

The Faithfulness of Jesus, God's Son (3:1–6)

In this section the author utilizes "synkrisis," or comparison, a rhetorical device common in both Greco-Roman literature and Jewish writings. In certain forms of rhetoric the point of such a comparison, rather than to disparage the comparable person (in this case Moses), is to

◀ *left*

RECEIPT FOR DELIVERY OF A SLAVE

This receipt is written on a pottery shard (*ostracon*) discovered in Egypt.

highlight the special status of the speech's main figure (in this case Christ).

Holy brothers, who share in the heavenly calling (3:1). At several points in Hebrews the author uses a noun (*metochos*) that the NIV translates here as a verb, "share" (1:9; 3:14; 6:4; 12:8). In the

▶
MICHELANGELO'S
STATUE OF MOSES

plural this word can be rendered companions, partakers, associates, or sharers. Ancient authors used the word to refer to a person in an especially close relationship or association. For instance, it could refer to a companion on a journey or a housemate. The Greek form of Ecclesiastes uses the word to translate 4:10: "If one falls down, his friend can help him up." The word is used widely to speak of business associates or those banded together by a common profession, and it also occurs in the context of persons sharing a meal or some form of instruction.[52] Hebrews uses the word to connote the close association formed around spiritual realities. The "heavenly calling" the hearers share gives them a firm basis for closeness of relationships in their community of faith.

Just as the builder of a house has greater honor (3:3). The construction of build-

▶ Moses

Moses was specially venerated in the Judaism of the first century A.D. In particular strands of Jewish tradition he is considered the greatest person of history, and a wealth of literature focuses on him as the main figure. Some teachings suggest that Moses held a greater status before God than the angels because of his special intimacy with God, seen in passages like Exodus 33:11: "The LORD would speak to Moses face to face, as a man speaks with his friend."[A-5] Sirach, a book in the Apocrypha, which dates from about 180 B.C., calls Moses:

> a godly man, who found favor in the sight of all and was beloved by God and people … [his] memory is blessed. He made him equal in glory to the holy ones, and made him great, to the terror of his enemies. By his words he performed swift miracles; the Lord glorified him in the presence of kings. He gave him commandments for

his people, and revealed to him his glory. For his faithfulness and meekness he consecrated him, choosing him out of all humankind. He allowed him to hear his voice, and led him into the dark cloud, and gave him the commandments face to face, the law of life and knowledge, so that he might teach Jacob the covenant, and Israel his decrees. (44:23–45:5)

Thus Moses' faithfulness to God was recognized and appreciated, as it is in Hebrews. Some interpreters expected the Messiah to come as a "new Moses," who would deliver his people. Note Deuteronomy 18:15–18, "The LORD your God will raise up for you a prophet like me from among your own brothers. …" The comparison in Hebrews 3, therefore, utilizes the great respect people had for Moses and makes a powerful case for an even greater honor as appropriate for Jesus.

ings and houses had reached the level of an art form in first-century Rome. The Romans started importing marble on a large scale at the beginning of the first century B.C. and, by the rise of Augustus, buildings such as the temple of Mars Ultor and the temple of Apollo Sosianus boasted marble walls or veneers. Builders also used stone, concrete, terra-cottas, wood, and bronze.

The housing industry thrived in the private sector as the emperors of the first century A.D. carried out impressive building campaigns in the public sector. Roman townhouses could be elaborate with dining rooms, a reception hall, and rooms for relaxation. The writer Vitruvius, in *The Ten Books on Architecture* (6.5.2), states that different types of houses were appropriate to persons of different classes:

> . . . for advocates and public speakers, handsomer and more roomy [houses], to accommodate meetings; for men of rank who, from holding offices and magistracies, have social obligations to their fellow-citizens, lofty entrance courts in regal style, and most spacious atria and peristyles, with plantations and walks of some extent in them, appropriate to their dignity. They need also libraries, picture galleries, and basilicas, finished in a style similar to that of great public buildings. . . .

At the apex of grand mansions was Nero's "Golden House," built after the great fire in Rome, which was a large villa in the middle of the city. His architect and engineer, Severus and Celer, are remembered for creating the triumph in a short span of time. These builders were famous for their work. As Hebrews notes, the builder of such a house has greater honor than the house itself.[53]

Hold on to our courage (3:6). The word translated "hold on to" (*katechō*) was used at times to mean "hold to, keep, detain, contain, occupy, or possess." Students of the era could be said to "hold to" a body of teaching. Hebrews uses the word to speak of holding to an identification with Christ, his teachings, and his community. The word translated "courage" (*parēssia*) communicates public boldness or the taking of a stand openly.

The Example of the Faithless Desert Wanderers (3:7–19)

The Exodus, in which faithful Moses led the Israelites from Egypt, and the subsequent desert wanderings constitute the most important era in the religious memory of the Jewish people. In a broad band of the Old Testament as well as in extrabiblical texts, the desert experience of the Israelites represents a paradigmatic symbol for disobedience to God.[54] Paul follows in this tradition:

> Now these things occurred as examples to keep us from setting our hearts on evil things as they did. Do not be idolaters, as some of them were. . . . We should not commit sexual immorality, as some of them did—and in one day twenty-three thousand of them died. We should not test the Lord, as some of them did—and were killed by snakes. And do not grumble, as some of them did—and were killed by the destroying angel.
>
> These things happened to them as examples and were written down as warnings for us, on whom the fulfillment of the ages has come. So, if you think you are standing firm, be careful that you don't fall![55]

Here in Hebrews 3 the author issues a stark warning to the hearers by quoting Psalm 95:7c–11. This passage was used liturgically as a preamble to synagogue services on Friday evenings and Sabbath mornings; thus the first hearers of Hebrews probably were familiar with the text. Some have suggested the psalm itself is a meditation on the desert rebellion recounted in Numbers 14.[56] In that chapter the Israelite spies have returned from their reconnaissance mission and, with the exception of Joshua and Caleb, have given their bad report to the people. The people weep and grumble against Moses and Aaron, insisting it would have been better to die in Egypt than to face the mighty enemies in the land of promise. They reject the godly men as leaders and threaten to stone them. The Lord takes this rebellion as an affront, a rejection and disbelief in himself. The tandem acts of disbelief and disobedience are especially egregious since God had worked mighty miracles in the congrega-tion's midst. The Lord says they have not listened to his voice (Num. 14:22) and, consequently, will not enter the Promised Land (14:30).

The methodology the author uses in this section is a form of *midrash* or running exposition on the Old Testament text. In midrash a rabbi cites and then explains a text on the basis of certain interpretative principles, often highlighting certain words as especially significant for his audience. Note how the author of Hebrews does this, taking the concepts "heart," "day," "today," "hear," "enter," "test," "rest," "unbelief," and "swear" from Psalm 95 and weaving them in a dynamic expositional exhortation.

A sinful, unbelieving heart (3:12). In biblical literature the "heart" is used metaphorically to refer to personality, intellect, memory, emotions, desires, or the will. On the negative side, the heart can be evil (1 Sam. 17:28), misguided (Jer. 17:9), or uncircumcised (Deut. 10:16; Jer. 9:26).

Hardness of heart refers to those who have set their wills against the will of the Lord.[57] Hebrews 3:12 makes this clear in that the hard heart is sinful and unbelieving (which the author practically equates with disobedience) and, consequently, turns away from the living God.

We have come to share in Christ if . . . (3:14). At a number of places in Paul's writings the apostle makes a statement of fact concerning the spiritual condition of his readers but then qualifies it. Romans 8:9, for instance, says, "You, however, are controlled not by the sinful nature but by the Spirit, if the Spirit of God lives in you." Similarly, Colossians 1:22–23 reads, "But now he has reconciled you by Christ's physical body through death to present you holy in his sight, without blemish and free from accusation—if you continue in your faith, established and firm, not moved from the hope held out in the gospel."[58] Our author does something similar in Hebrews 3:6, 14. He may have been influenced by Paul's writings or by the apostle himself in the use of this device.

Notice that in every case the author is dealing with a person's relationship with God. One explanation for this phenomenon is as follows. Paul and the author of Hebrews cannot look into a person's heart to see if faith is valid. Thus they are dependent on outward manifestations of inner spiritual realities.[59] The author of Hebrews cannot give unqualified assurance to those who may be turning away from God. Thus, he addresses the Christian community as a whole as those who "have come to share in Christ" but then qualifies that description as depending on one's perseverance in the faith. Such perseverance does not save but manifests the reality of one's salvation.

Who were they who heard and rebelled? (3:16). The question and answer format of 3:16–19 was a common rhetorical technique known as *subiectio*, in which an author or orator developed his message by asking and then answering a series of questions in rapid-fire succession.[60] In this passage the questions are taken from Psalm 95 and the answers from other Old Testament passages having to do with the desert rebellion.[61] It was a common feature of midrashic commentary to begin with a focal text and supplement a commentary on that text by referring to other, related texts. Thus the author draws on a broad range of Old Testament passages having to do with the rebellion in the desert to drive home the terrible

---

REFLECTIONS

THE HARDNESS OF HEART WITH which the author deals in Hebrews 3 stems from a pattern of life that turns a deaf ear to God's Word. The hardness may be thought of in terms of a spiritual callous that is built up by an action done time and again. A life characterized by disobedience, by neglect of one's relationship with God, becomes desensitized to God's voice. The actions we do day to day—even those that seem small infractions or slight aberrations on our moral landscape—compound over time when not dealt with appropriately. Thus, one of our most important spiritual exercises—indeed one that may determine the course of our very lives—is the practice of "hearing" God's voice daily through his Word, seeking to apply the truth consistently and repenting of sin.

price of disobedience to God. The format of question and answer provides a stylistic summary presenting the desert deserters as paradigmatic of that disobedience.

The Promise of God's Rest (4:1–11)

As is clear in the first three chapters of Hebrews, the author was a master of rabbinic techniques of interpretation and exposition, and one of the techniques he uses liberally is "verbal analogy." When using this method an ancient interpreter would bring two Scripture passages together that shared a common word or phrase, with the intention of elucidating one or both texts. In Hebrews 3:7–19 the focus is on Psalm 95, and the author concentrates on God's judgment for the wanderers' disobedience. In short, they were not allowed to enter God's rest. In 4:1–11 the author turns to a positive side of his exhortation—the promise of God's rest, which still stands for those who believe.

In commenting on God's "rest" the author introduces Genesis 2:2: "And on the seventh day God rested from all his work" (Heb. 4:4). Both Psalm 95 and Genesis 2:2 refer to God's rest, and, therefore, the writer of Hebrews brings these two passages together for consideration. From the word "today" in the psalm he concludes that God's rest is still available for his people (Heb. 4:1, 9). After all, David wrote the psalm years after the desert wanderers had passed from the scene and Joshua had led their children into the Promised Land (4:7–8). From the Genesis passage he reasons that God's rest involves ceasing from one's own works as God did from his (4:10), so it is a spiritual reality. Therefore, the writer encourages the hearers to make every effort to cease from their own works (i.e., enter God's rest) and not fall by following the example of the desert wanderers.

We who have believed enter that rest (4:3). The verb translated as "we who have believed" (*pisteuō*) occurs over two hundred times in the New Testament and is found in every book of the new covenant canon except Colossians, Philemon, 2 Peter, 2 and 3 John, and Revelation. The verb only occurs in Hebrews here and at 11:6, which is interesting given the author's emphasis on faith (esp. in ch. 11). In both the biblical literature generally and the secular literature of the Greco-Roman world the term can mean to be convinced of something or to believe someone. In religious contexts especially the word connotes trust. God or Christ is often the object, though the object may not be expressed at all, as here; rather, it is to be understood from the context. The exposition of Psalm 95 clearly shows that God is the object of belief or, in the case of the desert wanderers, the object of unbelief (Heb. 3:12, 19). Therefore, "we who have believed" refers to those who have placed their confidence in God, throwing their lot in with him.

Enter that rest ... seventh day ... Sabbath-rest (4:3–11). The concept of "rest" in Hebrews 4 has stimulated a good deal of discussion, with little consensus as the result. This concept forms an important motif in the Old Testament with various nuances. As is clear in Psalm 95, the "rest" can refer to entrance into the Promised Land of Canaan as the place of "resting" from bondage and wandering.[62] In Deuteronomy 12:9 this rest is coupled with the concept of inheritance of the land.

Genesis 2:2, which the author of Hebrews adds to his exposition at Hebrews 4:4, speaks of rest in terms of God's rest on the seventh day of creation. Both this verse from the Pentateuch and Psalm 95 speak of the rest as *God's* rest, and for our author this constitutes the connection between the two passages. Philo interpreted God's rest not as meaning that God ceased from his activity, but that God needed no effort for his continual work on the created order. Rather, he worked with such ease and skill as to continually be at rest.[63] Some rabbis also considered God's day of rest as open-ended—an eternal rest—since the creation account of the seventh day does not carry the refrain "and there was evening, and there was morning. . . ." For the author of Hebrews the emphasis is on the fact that God ceased from his works (Heb. 4:10).

Related directly to God's rest on the seventh day, the rest motif is also attached to the Sabbath Day and Sabbath festivals in the Old Testament.[64] The seventh day, grounded both in creation (Ex. 20:11) and in the deliverance from Egypt (Deut. 5:15), was to be a day of renewal as the devout Jew entered into God's rest. Festivals also could be referred to as "Sabbaths." Perhaps of significance for Hebrews 4, the Day of Atonement is said to be a "sabbath of rest."[65] The people were commanded to cease from work because the Lord made atonement for them. Hebrews 4 does not speak of the sacrifice of Christ specifically, but the author does mention the "gospel," which is to be heard with faith (4:1–2). Perhaps the ceasing from one's own works in Hebrews 4 is akin to Paul's concept of trusting God for covenant relationship.

"Rest" also could refer to the eternal or "eschatological" rest found at the end of one's life. This theme finds expression widely in extrabiblical Jewish literature. For instance, *Testament of Daniel* 5.12 speaks of the saints' rest they will find in Eden, which the author equates with the new Jerusalem, and *4 Ezra* 8:52 tells of a city that is built in paradise for the purpose of giving rest.

It may be suggested for Hebrews that the "rest" that those who believe have entered constitutes blessings of the "now" and the "not yet" of new covenant experience. We enter into a covenant Sabbath in which we, by faith, cease from our own works and persevere in trusting Christ's sufficiency for all our needs. Unlike the wanderers in the desert, we do not fall through unbelief. Yet, the concept of "rest" also seems to have a "not yet" component that focuses on our inheritance at the end of our pilgrimage. Thus we enter into the rest now, but will experience the consummation of full rest at the end of the age.

He spoke through David (4:7). The LXX, which is the author's translation of choice, specifically attributes Psalm 95 to

REFLECTIONS

WE LIVE IN A CULTURE DESPERATE FOR "REST." IT may be suggested that the root of the problem, rather than simply being physical exhaustion—a real issue in modern, Western culture—is a spiritual issue. We, as a culture, are much more oriented to human accomplishment than God's accomplishment on our behalf. Most turn away from God's works and God's ways, preferring, instead, life in the desert. As a believer, are you benefiting from God's promised rest today? Are you experiencing the peace and forgiveness provided for you under the new covenant, or is your life a spiritual frazzle? It may be that the lack of focus and the physical fatigue we experience has more to do with the state of our spirits than the fullness of our schedules.

David, the second king of Israel. That David penned the Psalm long after the passing of the deserters in the desert is significant for the author's argument (Heb. 4:7). Through David God implies that God's people may enter his rest by not following the example of disobedience recounted in the psalm. Even the fact that Joshua and the children entered the Promised Land does not mean that the promise of rest was thus fulfilled (4:8). Rather, as indicated by the word "today" in Psalm 95, God still offers an invitation to rest (Heb. 4:9). What Genesis 2 adds to the equation is that the rest offered constitutes ceasing from one's own works. For Hebrews this seems to be both a present and future reality.

A Warning Concerning God's Word (4:12–13)

The word of God is living and active (4:12). The beautifully crafted prose on God's word should be understood as echoing the reference to God's voice in the quotation of Psalm 95 (Heb. 3:7). First-century Judaism and Christianity both understood the word of God to be a force in creation, administration of the world, and judgment. The word, as indicated by the words "living and active," must not be thought of as static speech-act. Rather, it is a dynamic power that has the ability to effect change, both in the created order and in individual lives.

Sharper than any double-edged sword (4:12). The sword, ranging in size from sixteen inches to three feet, was the most basic weapon used in battle in the Greco-Roman world. For the first recipients of Hebrews the sight of a Roman soldier fully armored would have been common. As his primary weapon a Roman legionnaire would carry a *gladius*, a double-edged sword about twenty inches long, strapped to his right side. This weapon was designed for slashing and thrusting in close, hand-to-hand combat.[66]

Although the vast majority of the over four hundred references to a sword in Scripture refer to the literal weapon, it is used to symbolize war (e.g., Jer. 19:7; Hos. 2:18), bloodshed and conflict (e.g., 2 Sam. 12:10), and judgment, either human (Rom. 13:4) or divine (Ps. 7:12; Rev. 1:16). Negatively, the sword symbolizes anything that causes harm to people, such as destructive words (Ps. 57:4; Prov. 12:18), a false witness (Prov. 25:18), a sexually immoral woman (5:4), and the character of those who exploit the poor (30:14). Here in Hebrews 4:12 the author uses the image positively to speak of the power and effectiveness of God's Word (cf. Isa. 49:2; Eph. 6:17).[67] This "sword's" ability to cut deeply is seen in its penetration to a person's inner life. We might say that God's Word "gets to the heart" of any matter. In this sense it can be a powerful force of judgment when thoughts and intentions of the

THE "HOUSE OF DAVID" INSCRIPTION

A ninth-century B.C. Aramaic inscription found in Dan mentioning the battle of Ben Hadad, king of Aram, against "the house of David."

▼

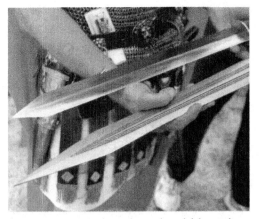

heart are not what they should be. Thus the author of Hebrews uses this image to warn against neglecting God's Word by failing to obey him.

Nothing in all creation is hidden from God's sight. Everything is uncovered and laid bare (4:13). The idea that the guilty were not able to hide from God's intense, penetrating judgment was common in Jewish theology of the era. In Revelation 6:16–17 those who face God's judgment wish to hide: "They called to the mountains and the rocks, 'Fall on us and hide us from the face of him who sits on the throne and from the wrath of the Lamb! For the great day of their wrath has come, and who can stand?'" Yet, of course, there is nowhere to hide from God. No one can

stand. The term translated in Hebrews 4:13 as "uncovered" (*gymnos*) normally connotes nakedness or lack of adequate clothing, but figuratively speaks of being vulnerable or helpless. Similarly, things that are "laid bare" are exposed and unprotected. So those who are disobedient to God, not attending to his voice, are vulnerable before his penetrating, judging Word.

A Capsule of the Author's Main Message (4:14–16)

Packed in these three verses we find the main elements of the author's message. We have a superior basis for holding onto our confession of Christ and drawing near to God. That superior basis is a relationship with Jesus, the Son of God, who functions as our great high priest. The passage forms the opening of an *inclusio* that the author closes at 10:19–25. An *inclusio* functioned to bracket a unit of text by marking its beginning and ending with an introduction and conclusion that were worded similarly. In this case the author marks the great central section on the Son's appointment to (5:1–10; 7:1–28), and ministry as (8:3–10:18), a superior high priest.

◀ *left*

DOUBLE-EDGED ROMAN SWORDS

Models of a Roman *gladius*.

▶Great High Priest

Under the old covenant the high priest was the chief leader in the worship of God and was the primary mediator between God and the nation. He is referred to variously as simply "the priest" (Ex. 31:10), "the anointed priest" (Lev. 4:3), "the chief priest" (2 Chron. 26:20), and the "high priest" (2 Kings 12:10). In the Pentateuch this last designation only occurs at Numbers 35:25–32; it also appears in Joshua 20:6. The appointment to high priesthood was hereditary and usually was an appointment for life.[A-6] The high priest had certain duties in common with other priests, but only he entered God's presence in the Most Holy Place on the Day of Atonement (Lev. 16:1–25).

Gone through the heavens (4:14). That Jesus has "gone through the heavens" simply means that he has entered God's presence. In the biblical literature "the heavens" can refer to the physical cosmos as distinct from the earth: "In the beginning God created the heavens and the earth" (Gen. 1:1). Biblical writers joined other peoples of the ancient world in describing the universe phenomenologically, that is, as they observed it. The heavens were above, the earth below. The physical heavens could be described as having a partition that God had "spread out" (Ps. 136:6; Isa. 42:5). Yet, the author of Hebrews is not primarily interested in Christ's physical journey through the cosmos but rather his going into the presence of the Father, and the imagery here has much to do with the exaltation theme already raised in the book (Heb. 1:3, 13). That he has "gone through the heavens" makes his passage into God's presence distinct from the earthly high priest, who entered God's presence through the earthly tabernacle (8:1–6; 9:1–10).

Jesus the Son of God (4:14). In the first chapters of Hebrews the author focused on Jesus as the "Son" of God. The designation of "son" or "sons of God" has a varied background in the Old Testament and Jewish literature. It could be used, for instance, of angels (e.g., Gen. 6:2; Job 1:6), the nation of Israel (Ex. 4:23), or the Davidic king (2 Sam. 7:12–14; 1 Chron. 17:13). *Wisdom of Solomon* 2:18 and *Sirach* 4:10, both Jewish writings of the Apocrypha, speak of the righteous person as "God's son." The latter reads: "Be a father to orphans, and be like a husband to their mother; you will then be like a son of the Most High, and he will love you more than does your mother."

The Dead Sea Scrolls, in a text from Cave 4 (4Q246), specifically refer to the Davidic Messiah, whose rule will be an eternal rule, as God's son:

All the peoples will serve him, and he shall become great upon the earth. . . . All will make peace, and all will serve him. He will be called son of the Great God; by His Name he shall be designated. He will be called the son of God; they will call him son of the Most High. . . . His Kingdom will be an Eternal Kingdom, and he will be Righteous in all his Ways.

Outside of Judaism, the title "son of God" is rare in the ancient Mediterranean world, and, "with one exception, is never used as a title."[68] That one exception is Augustus's adoption of the title *divi filius*, a Latin phrase translated on Greek inscriptions as *theou huios*, "son of God." But in no way should this be seen as the backdrop of the Christian use of the title, which takes its cues from the Old Testament and, especially, the title as used in Jesus' life and ministry.[69] For the author of Hebrews the title "Son of God" speaks of Jesus' unique relationship to God the Father, a relationship in which he reigns as Messiah and functions as our sinless, heavenly high priest.

Tempted in every way . . . yet was without sin (4:15). The confession that Jesus never sinned was common teaching in early Christian circles.[70] Matthew 4 and Luke 4 tell of the temptation of Jesus by the devil upon the launch of Jesus' ministry. The Lord answered those temptations with Scripture and won the day. That Jesus was tempted "in every way" and "was without sin" are important to the author's argument. The experience of temptation gives Jesus, as our high priest, a basis for sympathizing with us as human beings (a requirement of a

REFLECTIONS

DO YOU HAVE A SENSE OF CONFI-dence or boldness as you approach God in prayer? The clearer your picture of Jesus as high priest, the greater the confidence you will have. His sacrifice has opened the way completely for our access to God. What, then, are your needs for grace today? Bring those boldly to him now.

high priest, Heb. 5:1–3). Yet, his being without sin shows that Jesus is a high priest who is superior to the earthly priests, who had to offer sacrifices for themselves as well as the people (5:1–3; 7:26–28).

Let us then approach the throne of grace with confidence (4:16). Monarchs of the ancient world sat on thrones as symbols of their power and authority. Consequently, to approach a monarch's throne could be a fearsome act, for one was at the mercy of the ruler, who had the power of life and death in hand. The throne imagery also carried over into religious beliefs. For instance, a fresco from Pompeii depicts Bacchus (called Dionysus by the Greeks) sitting on a throne nude, with a wine cup in his right hand. When used with reference to the gods, a throne also was a symbol of power and authority. In Christian belief God's throne is a seat of authority and power, but, as Hebrews points out, it too is a seat of grace. Thus, the believer who has Christ as his high priest can approach the throne with "confidence" or boldness. In Hellenistic Judaism and early Christianity the concept of drawing near to God with confidence refers especially to approaching God in prayer.

An Introduction on Christ's Appointment as High Priest (5:1–10)

Hebrews 5:1–10 offers an introduction to a section running from 5:1 to 7:28 (with the exception of the strategic exhortation at 5:11–6:20). The author marks the section with a detailed *inclusio* (see introductory comments on 4:14–16), the opening of which occurs in 5:1–3 and the closing at 7:27–28. The content of 5:1–3 and 7:27–28, which demonstrate the contrast between Levitical priests and the priesthood of Christ, expresses the author's main concern. Specifically he addresses the theme of a high priest's appointment and shows that Jesus has been appointed in a superior fashion as a superior high priest. At the heart of this agenda lies Psalm 110:4: "You are a priest forever, in the order of Melchizedek."

Every high priest (5:1). Both the Greeks and Romans had organizations of priests who had various functions, including the offering of sacrifices to the gods. For example, the Romans had The College of

HIGH PRIEST

An artistic representation of the Jewish high priest in his vestments.

Priests, a group of sixteen who controlled the ritual practices of the religious calendar. Other Roman groups were the flamines, the Vestal Virgins, and the augurs, all of which had different functions.[71] But Hebrews' orientation is strictly to the Old Testament and the priesthood as described in its pages. The first four verses of Hebrews 5 delineate universal principles on high priesthood gleaned from that source.

First, the high priest has a relationship of solidarity with the people because he is appointed "from among" them (5:1). It may be that this principle derives from Exodus 28:1, which says that Aaron was brought to Moses "from among the Israelites."

Second, the high priest represents people by joining the other priests in offering sacrifices to God (Heb. 5:1). Yet, the high priest alone offers the sacrifice on the Day of Atonement (Ex. 29:1–46; Lev. 16:1–25). The Day of Atonement sacrifice involved two goats and a ram. One of the goats was slaughtered as a sin offering, and the other was the "scapegoat," which the high priest, having laid hands on its head and confessing the sins of the people, sent into the desert (Lev. 16:15, 20–22).

Third, on the Day of Atonement the high priest also was required to offer a sacrifice for himself and his household before he offered the sacrifice for the people (5:3; cf. Lev. 16:11). The reason for this sacrifice was to deal with his own weakness (Heb. 5:2). His weaknesses, however, play a significant role in his ministry since they enable him to "deal gently with those who are ignorant and are going astray" (5:2).

A fourth general principle concerns how one becomes a high priest. It is not by enlisting, but rather by being appointed by God (5:1, 4)[72]. Thus the basis for the position of high priest rests in the authority of God, not people. These four principles lay the foundation for the author's understanding of Jesus' unique service as high priest.

Gifts and sacrifices for sins (5:1). Neighbors who participated in religious sacrifices to various degrees certainly surrounded the first recipients of Hebrews. Sacrifices were made primarily to get what one wanted or to protect one from some harm. Thus the sacrifices were expressions of self-centered superstition. Also, in Greek and Roman religion there was a great emphasis on the exact performance of such rituals. In fact, if a ceremony or sacrifice was not executed in exactly the right manner, the process had to be started again. The gods were the strictest sort of legalists in the Greco-Roman understanding of things.

The gifts and sacrifices Hebrews 5:1 mentions are quite different because they center on relationship with God. The sacrifices of the old covenant system included the burnt offering, the sin offering, the guilt offering, and the thank offering (Lev. 1–7), each in its own way addressing one's relationship with God. The Day of Atonement sacrifice, offered on the tenth day of the seventh month (September/October), was the most important sacrifice and is the primary sacrifice in mind here. This sacrifice covered all of the sins not covered in the previous year by other sacrifices. On this day the people drew near to God by the high priest's entering the Most Holy Place. The temple sacrifices continued through most of the New Testament era but ceased after the destruction of the temple by the Romans in A.D. 70.

A priest forever, in the order of Melchizedek (5:6). The quotation of Psalm 110:4 here introduces the discussion of Jesus' superior appointment as a priest, a topic that will govern the author's arguments in Hebrews 7:1–28. The proclamation of the Davidic king as "a priest forever, in the order of Melchizedek" has its background in David's conquest of Jerusalem about a thousand years before the birth of Christ. As a consequence of that victory, David and his descendants became heirs of Melchizedek's dynasty of priest-kings.[73] Jesus and his first followers understood this psalm to be a prophecy concerning the Messiah, and the author of Hebrews is especially focused on the fact that Psalm 100 shows that Jesus, as Messiah, was appointed priest by a divine proclamation.

Prayers and petitions with loud cries and tears (5:7). The wording of Hebrews 5:7 seems to echo Jesus' agonizing submission to his Father in Gethsemane.[74] Yet, it should be noted that the Gospel accounts do not mention "cries and tears," and, consequently, scholars have sought to ascertain the background of the author's reflections on these expressions of grief. The early Christians meditated on the psalms as predictive of the life, suffering, and exaltation of Jesus. The psalms of "righteous suffering" probably form the backdrop of the "cries and tears" of Hebrews 5:7.

Although he was a son, he learned obedience from what he suffered and, once made perfect (5:8–9). Paul noted that the crucifixion of Jesus was a stumbling block to the Jews and foolishness to the Gentiles (1 Cor. 1:23). That God's Son should die a shameful death by the most base form of execution was outside the bounds of all expectation in both Jewish

---

▶ Psalms of Righteous Suffering

Psalm 116:1–8 declares:

> I love the LORD, for he heard my voice;
>   he heard my cry for mercy....
>
> The cords of death entangled me,
>   the anguish of the grave came upon me;
> I was overcome by trouble and sorrow....
>
> You, O LORD, have delivered my soul from death,
>   my eyes from tears,
>   my feet from stumbling.

Psalm 22, a messianic psalm of suffering (cf. the author's quote of Ps. 22:22 at Heb. 2:12), reads:

> My God, my God, why have you forsaken me?
>   Why are you so far from saving me,
>   so far from the words of my groaning?
> O my God, I cry out by day, but you do not answer,
>   by night, and am not silent. (2:1–2)

> My strength is dried up like a potsherd,
>   and my tongue sticks to the roof of my
>   mouth;
>   you lay me in the dust of death. (2:15)
>   Revere him, all you descendants of Israel!
> For he has not despised or disdained
>   the suffering of the afflicted one;
> he has not hidden his face from him
>   but has listened to his cry for help. (2:23b–24)

When Hebrews says that the Father heard the Son's cry because of his reverent submission, it reflects a key value of Jewish piety, that is, humble submission to God's will. Also, that God the Father affirms Jesus in his suffering ultimately is seen in the resurrection and exaltation, twin events that vindicate Jesus as the Messiah.

and Greek cultures. Sons of high position in the ancient world were honored and advanced on the basis of their status. Yet Jesus' relationship with the Father did not make for an easy appointment to high priesthood.

That Jesus "learned obedience" does not mean that he was disobedient and then became obedient. Rather, it means that Jesus followed fully and obediently the path of suffering the Father had designed for him. He experienced fully what it meant to be in complete submission to the Father. Also, his being "made perfect" relates to the completion of his course of suffering—not that he was imperfect before, but he "ran the full course" of his sufferings and thus became fully qualified as our high priest.

The Spiritual Immaturity of the Recipients (5:11–14)

In ancient rhetoric a sudden shift of topic could be used strategically to rivet the audience's attention. This is what the author of Hebrews does at 5:11. He departs momentarily from a discussion of Jesus' appointment as a priest like Melchizedek to confront the hearers with their spiritual lethargy. The language used in this passage was common in educational circles of the Mediterranean.

Slow to learn (5:11). The Greek expression here means "dull of hearing." The first word in the phrase, *nōthroi*, can mean "sluggish, dull, dimwit, negligent," or "lazy." For instance, Plutarch notes that Parmenion was sluggish and lazy in battle; the term could also be used of an athlete who was slow because he was out of shape physically.[75] In both the Wisdom literature and Greek literature generally,

the word connotes the failure to follow through with work or a responsibility because of being dull or slow in some aspect of life.[76] Specifically the author links the laziness of the recipients of Hebrews to "hearing," since he is concerned that they are failing to give full attention to God's Word.

Elementary truths of God's word (5:12). The word rendered "elementary truths" (*stoicheia*) means "basic principles" and can refer to spiritual beings of the universe in more metaphysical contexts.[77] But another use of the word in ancient literature comes closer to the author's use here. Writers used *stoicheia* to refer to basic elements of the alphabet or the most basic, fundamental concepts in education.[78] Thus, we might, with the NEB translation, think of the term as used in Hebrews 5:12 as meaning "the ABCs of God's Word." The author of Hebrews is concerned that the hearers, who have been believers long enough to be advanced in the faith, have stagnated at, or even digressed to, a point of gross immaturity.

You need milk, not solid food (5:12). In educational contexts the imagery of "milk and solid food" was a common means of delineating basic from ad-

right ▶

GREEK "ABC'S"

A potsherd (*ostracon*) used in a Greek writing exercise.

vanced teachings. The rabbis sometimes called their young students "sucklings."[79] Epictetus, a crippled Greek slave during the reign of Nero, uses the milk/meat imagery to comment on the immaturity of the person who demands life be a certain way in order to be happy. He states, "Are you not willing, at this late date, like children, to be weaned and to partake of more solid food, and not to cry for mammies and nurses—old wives' lamentations?" Having challenged the young man to get out into the world and taste widely of the challenges God brings in life, he laments, "Nay, you will not; sit rather in the house as girls do and wait for your mammy until she feeds you!"[80] Speaking of education, Philo of Alexandria writes that milk is the food of babies and suited for the time of childhood (i.e., the beginning stages of education), but grown men should partake of more substantial fare that leads to wisdom, self-control, and virtue.[81]

The concern expressed by the writer of Hebrews is that this community of believers evidences a staggering lack of maturity. They should be much farther down the road of faith and should be assimilating advanced teachings of the Christian life (e.g., the high priesthood of Christ), but they rather need to have their attention refocused on the most basic teachings of Christ (cf. 2:1).

By constant use (5:14). By contrast, those who are mature can handle "solid food," because of their spiritual condition. The term translated by the NIV with "constant use" (*hexis*) has been widely mistranslated and misinterpreted as referring to "exercise" or "practice" of one's spiritual faculties. The term refers rather to the "condition" or "state" of the mature person. It is because of their

REFLECTIONS

DO YOU SEE A PATTERN OF GROWTH in your own life by which you are moving from the need of "milk" to the spiritual intake of "meat"? Would you say that the past year of your Christian life has been characterized by progression in understanding Christian teachings or by stagnation? Notice that growth in this passage is tied to *teachings* about Christ. Theology, in a real sense, lays the foundation for living. In other words, right thinking leads to right living. As we grow in character, however, we grow in our ability to grasp deeper truths of the faith.

mature condition that the mature have the faculties to discern good and evil.

A Challenge to Move on in the Faith (6:1–3)

Let us leave the elementary teachings about Christ (6:1). In 5:11–14 the author has pointed out that there are those in the church he addresses who have stagnated spiritually, needing remedial work on Christian teachings. But he does not accede to their infantile appetites; rather, he challenges them to move on in the faith. Early Christianity seems to have borrowed from Judaism the practice of using catechisms for instructing new converts or young believers. Most foundational materials certainly pointed to the Old Testament Scriptures as providing the basics of Christian faith. Therefore, the items that follow, although cornerstones of basic Jewish teaching in the era, had been assimilated as basics of Christian belief and could only be seen as foundational. To stay at the level of those most basic beliefs constituted immaturity. Nevertheless, the author's listing of these basic theological concepts shows their importance in the basic teachings of the first-century church.

The foundation of repentance from acts that lead to death, and of faith in God (6:1). Repentance and faith are two of the most basic elements of Jewish and Christian teachings of the first century. Some commentators have suggested that this first pair of concepts in the author's list of 6:1–3 lays the foundation for the other two pairs. Those two pairs, baptisms and laying on of hands, and resurrection from the dead and eternal judgment, relate to the beginning and end, respectively, of the life of faith. Yet, the beginning point of everything is to repent of sins and to have faith in God. The *Didache*, a collection of Christian teachings written after Hebrews, tells of the "way of death," which involves sins such as murder, adultery, lust, fornication, robbery, idolatry, magic, hypocrisy,

and arrogance. In Romans 6:21 Paul notes that the outcome of slavery to the life of sin is death.[82] Death, however, can be avoided by genuine repentance. What corresponds to genuine repentance is faith in God, and the relationship between repentance and faith can be seen readily in the preaching both of Jesus and Paul. Jesus called people to "repent and believe the good news" (Mark 1:15), and Paul gave these twin concepts as the essence of his gospel (Acts 20:21).

Instruction about baptisms (6:2). The term "baptisms," as indicated by the NIV translation, is plural, and thus challenges the interpretation that the author simply has in mind Christian baptism. The act of religious washings was prevalent in first-century Judaism. The Qumran community (the writers of the Dead Sea Scrolls), for instance, had "baptisms" for those who were joining their group; they also had subsequent washings so that ritual purity could be maintained. Excavations near the caves where the Dead Sea Scrolls were found include pools and containers that may have been used for such washings. Some wealthy, devout Jews in the city of Jerusalem had pools in their home for ritual cleansing. The Pharisees took the hand washings done by the Levitical priests and applied them generally to ritual purity before eating.

Yet it may be that the author's primary reference point is the Old Testament writings. In 9:13 and 10:22 the author refers to the cleansing ceremonies of the old covenant. These washings are presented as inadequate from a Christian perspective, though they do have significance in foreshadowing the cleansing offered by Christ's superior new covenant offering.

BAPTISMAL POOL

A *miqveh* from the southern wall excavations just south of the Temple Mount in Jerusalem.

▼

The laying on of hands (6:2). In the New Testament the laying on of hands is associated with ritual blessing (e.g., Matt. 19:13, 15), healing of the sick (e.g., Mark 5:22–23; Luke 4:40; 13:13), the initial ministry of the Holy Spirit in a new convert's life (e.g., Acts 8:17–19), and the authorization or, perhaps, the acknowledgement of a particular ministry (e.g., 6:6; 13:3). In line with the context of Hebrews 6:2, the book of Acts shows that the laying on of hands sometimes accompanied baptism in early Christian circles (Acts 8:16–17; 19:5–6). Significantly for the broader context of Hebrews, the practice of the laying on of hands also relates to the old covenant sacrificial system, most notably the act of the high priest, who laid his hands on the scapegoat on the Day of Atonement.

The resurrection from the dead, and eternal judgment (6:2). Resurrection from the dead and eternal judgment are linked together in the biblical literature and extrabiblical, Jewish writings. The raising of the dead results in new life and reward for those who are righteous and judgment for the wicked. Isaiah 26:19 tells of the resurrection of the righteous, for instance, and Daniel 12:2 includes resurrection for the righteous and the wicked. Sources such as 2 Maccabees 7 and *2 Baruch* 49–51 speak of physical resurrection to a bodily existence. In the rabbinic writings resurrection refers to God's bringing all the dead, righteous and unrighteous, back to life on the Day of Judgment. With the decline of the sect of the Sadducees and the firm control of Pharisaic Judaism after the destruction of the temple in A.D. 70, the doctrine was fixed in broader Jewish thought. In *m. Sanhedrin* 10:1 those who do not believe that the doctrine of the resurrection has

its origin in the Torah have no place in the coming age.[83] Jesus himself chastised the Sadducees for their lack of understanding of the resurrection, doing so by pointing to the Torah (Luke 20:37–38): "But in the account of the bush, even Moses showed that the dead rise, for he calls the Lord 'the God of Abraham, and the God of Isaac, and the God of Jacob.' He is not the God of the dead, but of the living, for to him all are alive."

A Harsh Warning Against Falling Away (6:4–6)

It is impossible for those who have once been enlightened (6:4). The word "impossible" is positioned at the beginning of the Greek sentence beginning with 6:4, and, based on a principle from Greek grammar, the author wishes to place emphasis on this term. Elsewhere in Hebrews the word is used to refer to something that cannot happen. In 6:18 we are told that God cannot lie, in 10:4 that the blood of bulls and goats cannot take away sins, and in 11:6 that it is impossible to please God apart from faith.

Broadly in the writings of the ancient world, the word translated "enlightened" served as a metaphor for making known what was previously unknown. In writers such as Plato, Plutarch, Aristotle, and Sophocles, those who gained some form of knowledge are called "enlightened." More specifically "light" is connected to the world of the gods; in the Old Testament it is associated with the one true God (Ps. 4:6; 89:15; Dan. 2:22). Philo describes right teaching or thought as "the light of thought," the "light of the spirit," or "the light of truth."[84]

Who have tasted the goodness of the word of God (6:5). The concept of "tasting" here has at times been misinterpreted to mean "partially ingested," but this understanding cannot hold up to scrutiny. Rather, as in Jesus' tasting death in 2:9, to taste something means to experience it. To "taste the goodness of the word of God" perhaps follows from the "spiritual food" imagery of 5:11–14 and recalls the exhortation of Psalm 34:8, "Taste and see that the LORD is good," and the exultation of 119:103, "How sweet are your words to my taste!"

And the powers of the coming age (6:5). In Jewish thought "this age" constitutes the period from creation to the Day of Judgment. The "coming age" follows the final judgment of God and will see God's total rule consummated. For Paul, the present age is evil and ruled by the evil powers (1 Cor. 2:6; Gal. 1:4). That those spoken of in Hebrews 6:5 have tasted "the powers of the coming age" means that in some way they have experienced the effects of God's rule, which will be experienced ultimately in the age to come—his powerful intervention in humanity, his breaking the evil powers of this evil age.

If they fall away (6:6). The word rendered "fall away" recalls the "drifting" of 2:1 and the warning against a heart that "turns away" in 3:12. The image draws most, however, from the desert wanderers who "fell" and were not able to enter the Promised Land (3:17; 4:11). Telling of God's judgment on the wanderers, Numbers 14:29–30 reads, "In this desert your bodies will fall—every one of you twenty years old or more who was counted in the census and who has grumbled against me. Not one of you will enter the land I swore with uplifted hand to make your home, except Caleb son of

Jephunneh and Joshua son of Nun" (cf. Ps. 106). The verb used in Hebrews 6:6, used only here in the New Testament, occurs in contexts in the LXX in which unfaithfulness is in view (e.g., Ezek. 14:13; 15:8).

They are crucifying the Son of God all over again and subjecting him to public disgrace (6:6). In 13:13 the author notes the proper stance of a Christian, a stance that constitutes standing with Christ, bearing his disgrace. Thus believers are challenged to follow the example of the Lord, who "scorned [the] shame" of the cross (12:2). The apostates used as a negative example in Hebrews 6:4–8, however, have reversed this position, instead standing with those who used the cross, the ultimate instrument of public shame in the Greco-Roman world, to crucify Christ. Crosses often were placed on main thoroughfares so that the victim would be publicly humiliated. Matthew 27:39–44 vividly recounts the shaming of Christ:

> Those who passed by hurled insults at him, shaking their heads and saying, "You who are going to destroy the temple and build it in three days, save yourself! Come down from the cross, if you are the Son of God!"
> In the same way the chief priests, the teachers of the law and the elders mocked him. "He saved others," they said, "but he can't save himself! He's the King of Israel! Let him come down now from the cross, and we will believe in him. He trusts in God. Let God rescue him now if he wants him, for he said, 'I am the Son of God.'" In the same way the robbers who were crucified with him also heaped insults on him.

An Agricultural Image of Blessing and Judgment (6:7–8)

The agricultural image contrasting good ground and poor ground was common in the ancient world. Many ancient societies were oriented to agriculture, and ground that failed to produce was seen as a curse. Such ground often was burned off. The image forms the backdrop, for example, of the Song of the Vineyard in Isaiah 5:1–7 and of Jesus' parable of the sower (Matt. 13:1–9; Mark 4:3–9). Those who have rejected Christ, failing to bear the fruit of faith, correspond to ground that has failed to produce anything worthwhile, in spite of favorable conditions. The inevitable outcome of such people is devastation.

In Greek culture curses were hostile prayers that at times were scratched on tablets called *defixiones*, addressed to the gods of the underworld and placed in the ground, in wells, or in graves.[85] In biblical literature blessings and curses for the most part, rather than referring to a magical incantation, refer to the good gifts of God over against tragic circumstances that result from unfaithfulness. Blessings and curses, therefore, can be formal statements of good or ill fortune, visited on people in response to their actions. For example, in Deuteronomy 27:15–29:1 the Lord gives the Israelites the terms of the covenant. If they follow the Lord's commandments, faithfully fulfilling the covenant, a whole host of blessings will be lavished on them. However, if they forsake the Lord's commands, rejecting the terms of the covenant, they will be cursed with a long list of curses. The agricultural image of Hebrews 6:7–8 is analogous to this concept. The land that produces good fruit receives God's blessing or favor. The land that does not produce (failing to be faithful to the covenant?) faces an inevitable curse.

Further Encouragement (6:9–12)

Dear friends (6:9). The author softens the harshness of the previous negative example (6:4–6) and agricultural figure (6:7–8) with a reference to his hearers as "dear friends." The verb form of this word, *agapaō*, was used at times in Greek literature to mean "greet with affection," and the use of the word *agapētos* in 6:9, as indicated by the NIV, is meant to be an affectionate greeting.

We are confident of better things in your case (6:9). Expressing confidence in an audience or recipients of a letter was a rhetorical device used to create a sense of obligation or to persuade those addressed to take a certain course of action. Paul uses the device to good effect, for instance, at Romans 15:14: "I myself am convinced, my brothers, that you yourselves are full of goodness, complete in knowledge and competent to instruct one another."

HARVEST

A modern harvest of vegetables in Jordan near the Dead Sea.

He will not forget your work (6:10). God is a God who remembers. In the Old Testament God "remembers his covenant" he made with his people.[86] In an interesting contrast to Hebrews 6:10, Ezekiel 18:24 states, "But if a righteous man turns from his righteousness and commits sin and does the same detestable things the wicked man does, will he live? None of the righteous things he has done will be remembered. Because of the unfaithfulness he is guilty of and because of the sins he has committed, he will die." This is not the situation under the new covenant, however. The faith of the hearers of Hebrews has been lived out in "work," a manifestation of love for God expressed through ministry to others. The description points to genuine relationship with God, a relationship manifested by good works and ministry to the saints.[87] Thus, unlike the negative examples of Hebrews 6:4–8, they have been fruitful, good "ground."

Imitate those who through faith and patience inherit what has been promised (6:12). The theme of imitation is one that occurs consistently in Paul's writings and anticipates both the treatment of Abraham in the next few verses and, especially, the great list of the faithful in chapter 11.[88] The pattern common to those whom the author has in mind, is a life of faith, exercised in patience, that leads ultimately to God's fulfillment of his promises. This is the great story of the Bible. God has promised; his people must wait for the answer; the answer, in accordance with the character of God, follows the life of faith.

The Power of God's Promises (6:13–20)

The whole of 6:13–20 is transitional, leading back to the discussion on Melchizedek from which the author temporarily departed at 5:11. God's oath, or promise, constitutes the author's main topic for discussion. The passage progresses along the lines of an illustration (6:13–15), followed by a truism (6:16) and then the main point (6:17–18).

When God made his promise to Abraham (6:13). In Jewish culture of the first century, Abraham was the example par excellence of faithful perseverance since he persevered in believing God for a son and then was willing to sacrifice that son in obedience to God. The key here is that God swore an oath to Abraham, saying, "I will surely bless you and make your descendants . . . numerous" (Gen. 22:17); the context of this verse recounts the near sacrifice of Isaac. In an obedient response to God's oath Abraham waited on God's timing and received the promise (Heb. 6:15). The author wishes to stress that Abraham did well because he believed God's oath. This is the point of the illustration.

Men swear by someone greater than themselves (6:16). The writer of Hebrews here offers a truism, or universal truth; the language used in this passage is taken right out of the legal contexts of the day. The author points out that oaths taken in a court of law or a legal situation have two characteristics. First, they require that the oath-giver appeal to a superior. The superior lends the oath-giver credibility, a credibility founded in the character of the superior. Second, witnesses swear an oath as a means of giving a legal guarantee of the truthfulness of their words. This is a "confirmation" that what they are saying is true. When the testimony of the witness comes to this point, room for dispute no longer exists.

Another area in which an oath gave assurance was that of contractual relationships, especially verbal ones. The *Ius iurandum liberti*, for example, was an oath given by a recently freed slave. The new freedman swore an oath to render services to his patron promised prior to his liberation.[89] Thus, the oath served as a guarantee that such services would be forthcoming. Philo comments on such oath-giving in human relationships, "Matters that are in doubt are decided by an oath, insecure things made secure, assurance given to that which lacked it."[90] The author of Hebrews reasons in Hebrews 6:17 that if oaths give assurance in courts of law or legal situations where human beings are involved, God's oath can be counted on as an even greater confirmation of truth.

By two unchangeable things in which it is impossible for God to lie (6:18). The "two unchangeable things" of 6:18 are the two parts of Psalm 110:4, to which the author alludes: "You are a priest forever" and "in the order of Melchizedek." The allusion as used here begins a transition back to a discussion of Melchizedek in chapter 7. In that chapter the author expounds the two parts of Psalm 110:4 in inverse order:

> "You are a priest forever" (Heb. 7:15–28).
> "In the order of Melchizedek" (Heb. 7:11–14).

Why are these two proclamations by God "unchangeable"? In the words of Psalm 110:4, "The LORD has sworn and will not change his mind." God cannot lie (Heb. 6:18).

Fled to take hold of the hope (6:18). Although the concept of fleeing to a refuge has parallels in Greek literature

(e.g., Plato, *Theaet.* 176A-B), the motif is a common one in the Old Testament. Generally speaking, God is the believer's refuge, to whom the believer can go in times of trouble (e.g. Ps. 144:2), and those who take refuge in God will inherit the land (Isa. 57:13). The "cities of refuge" were for those who had accidentally killed someone; such cities provided a safe place from revenge taken by the victim's family.[91]

It seems that the author combines two Old Testament themes in his imagery here, themes related to the horns of the altar. First, at the end of God's instructions concerning the altar of incense (Ex. 30:1–10), the horns of the altar are said to have a special role in the Day of Atonement. Speaking of the altar, the writer says, "Once a year Aaron shall make atonement on its horns. This annual atonement must be made with the blood of the atoning sin offering for the generations to come. It is most holy to the LORD." Exodus 30:6, moreover, makes it clear that the altar was to be located in front of the veil separating the outer room of the sanctuary from the inner room (the author of Hebrews understands the altar to be inside the Most Holy Place; see 9:3–4). Second, in 1 Kings 1:50–53 Adonijah fled to take hold of the horns of the altar as a place of safety from Solomon's wrath and was spared (Joab, whom Solomon deemed guilty, attempted the same but was not so fortunate; 1 Kings 2:28–35). Thus, believers have fled to take hold of the hope—the "horns of the altar" where atonement has been made for sins through Jesus' high priestly offering (see also Lev. 16:18). This hope, therefore, enters "behind the curtain" (6:19) and gives us a place of refuge.

An anchor for the soul, firm and secure (6:19). Plato said the cities of Greece were clustered on the shores of the Mediterranean "like frogs on a pond," and the Romans referred to that body of water as "our Sea."[92] The strong orientation to this large, central body of water was due to the importance of shipping as a primary mode of transportation for both Greeks and Romans. Ships served mainly to carry grain, oil, and wine, but people could buy passage to different locations at certain times of the year. Therefore, ancient peoples were familiar with nautical imagery, and the anchor was a common philosophical metaphor representing stability. For instance, the Greek philosopher Plutarch, who lived in the first Christian century, criticizes those who cannot control their desires, saying, "The spirit yields and can resist no more, like an anchor-hook in sand amid the surge."[93] In other words, a person who gives in to passions is no more stable than an anchor in sand. Philo uses the image of an anchor when speaking of virtue as a stabilizer in life. To have virtue is like being anchored in a safe place.[94]

Hebrews uses the anchor imagery to emphasize that believers have a firm basis for spiritual security. The word translated "secure" refers to something that is reliable, well-founded, or confirmed. So our hope in Christ, rather than based on emotions or wishful thinking, provides a firm basis for a life of stability.

The inner sanctuary behind the curtain (6:19). The tabernacle of the Israelites was a network of curtains made in part of fine twisted linen (Ex. 26:1) and a series of boards made of acacia wood (26:15–30). The tabernacle was divided into two rooms, an outer room (the Holy Place) that contained the lampstand and the table holding the bread of the Presence (25:23–40), and the Most Holy Place or inner room, which contained the ark of the covenant (25:10–22). Separating the two rooms was a "curtain," and God commanded the following concerning this curtain:

> Make a curtain of blue, purple and scarlet yarn and finely twisted linen, with cherubim worked into it by a skilled craftsman. Hang it with gold hooks on four posts of acacia wood overlaid with gold and standing on four silver bases. Hang the curtain from the clasps and place the ark of the Testimony behind the curtain. The curtain will separate the Holy Place from the Most Holy Place (Ex. 26:31–33).

For the author of Hebrews, the Christian's hope is to enter the inner sanctuary behind the curtain because that is where Jesus has gone as our high priest.

▶

STONE ANCHOR

In the old covenant religion, only the high priest could enter the inner sanctuary, and he could do so only once a year on the Day of Atonement. Jesus, however, has entered the true Most Holy Place, heaven, and there intercedes always for us (Heb. 7:25). Thus our hope is made as sure as it could be, Jesus providing a superior, lasting covenant that guarantees our permanent audience with the living God.

He has become a high priest forever, in the order of Melchizedek (6:20). In 6:20 the author now cites overtly what he has alluded to in 6:17–18, restating the content of Psalm 110:4 (Heb. 5:6). These two parts of this Psalm verse, that Jesus is a priest forever and is in the order of Melchizedek, constitute the two main themes of 7:11–28.

The Superiority of Melchizedek (7:1–10)

Hebrews 7 picks up on the topic introduced in 5:1–10—Jesus' appointment as high priest—and presents a tightly woven argument built around the enigmatic, Old Testament figure Melchizedek. There are only two references in the Old Testament to this "priest of God": Genesis 14:17–20 and Psalm 110:4. The first gives the narrative recounting Abraham's meeting with Melchizedek after the patriarch's return from battle and is the focal text for Hebrews 7:1–10. Psalm 110:4, on the other hand, offers a reflection on the Davidic monarch, whose priesthood is enduring (see comments on Heb. 6:18).

The type of commentary found in 7:1–10 is known as *midrash* (see comments on 3:7–19). J. A. Fitzmyer has noted that Hebrews 7 has features in common with a midrash: The Old Testament text is the point of departure, the exposition is homiletical, the author stresses details of the scriptural passage, the text is shown to be relevant to the contemporary audience, and the focus is on the narrative of the Old Testament situation, not just the individual characters.[95]

This Melchizedek (7:1). The author of Hebrews may have been familiar with

---

▶ What Jews in the Greco-Roman Era Thought About Melchizedek

Extrabiblical literature prior to, during, and following the advent of Christianity shows an interest in the figure of Melchizedek. Philo mentions him at several places, mostly using him as a symbol, for instance, of the Logos.[A-7]

The Qumran community had an interest in the priest as a heavenly figure, as shown by a Dead Sea scroll fragment on Melchizedek found in Cave 11, which dates from around the time of Christ's birth. The fragment interprets, among other texts, Leviticus 25:9–13, a passage dealing with the Jubilee Year. In the Qumran fragment the last Jubilee is called the "Year of Melchizedek," in which Melchizedek is said to bring deliverance and salvation to the people of God by defeating Belial and his evil spirits. 11QMel ii.13 states, "And Melchizedek will exact the ven[geance] of E[l's] judgments [and he will protect all the sons of light from the power] of Belial and from the power of all [the spirits of] his [lot]." Melchizedek is apparently some type of heavenly figure in this scroll fragment, perhaps an exalted angel.[A-8]

In the first-century work *2 Enoch* Melchizedek also is a heavenly figure. Here Melchizedek is saved from the flood so he can continue a line of priests started with Seth. Michael takes the child Melchizedek to paradise, where he is to be a priest forever.[A-9]

speculations about Melchizedek in various religious communities of his day. Yet, the author's treatment of this priest can be explained wholly on his treatment of the two Old Testament texts in which Melchizedek is named. His treatment of Melchizedek in 7:1–10 can be explained as an exposition of Genesis 14:17–20 with Psalm 110:4 in mind.

He met Abraham returning from the defeat of the kings (7:1). Melchizedek was a priest-king from the city of Salem. He met Abraham as the patriarch was returning from an important victory over a confederation of four kings from the east: Kedorlaomer of Elam, Tidal of Goiim, Amraphel of Shinar, and Arioch of Ellasar. These four kings had attacked the kings of Sodom, Gomorrah, Admah, Zeboiim, and Bela, defeating them at the Valley of Siddim and plundering their cities. Abraham's nephew Lot was taken captive from Sodom. Upon hearing of his nephew's plight, Abraham pursued the invaders to the city of Dan, where he won the victory in a nighttime attack. On his way back home, the king of Sodom and Melchizedek met the patriarch, at which time Abraham gave the latter a tenth of his spoils and Melchizedek blessed him. Genesis 14:17–20 says this about Melchizedek:

> After Abram returned from defeating Kedorlaomer and the kings allied with him, the king of Sodom came out to meet him in the Valley of Shaveh (that is, the King's Valley).
> Then Melchizedek king of Salem brought out bread and wine. He was priest of God Most High, and he blessed Abram, saying,
>
> "Blessed be Abram by God Most High,

> Creator of heaven and earth.
> And blessed be God Most High,
> who delivered your enemies into your hand."

Then Abram gave him a tenth of everything.

His name means (7:2). In dealing with Melchizedek's name the author of Hebrews alludes to words from the Hebrew language. When he suggests his name means "king of righteousness," the reference is to the Hebrew words *melek*, which means "king," and *sedeq*, which may be rendered "righteousness." The city name "Salem," furthermore, he interprets to mean "peace," drawing an association between the city's name and the Hebrew word *shalom*.

Without father or mother, without genealogy, without beginning of days or end of life (7:3). A common exegetical practice from the era may be called "an argument from silence"; the author uses this technique, pointing out what the Old Testament passage *does not* say about Melchizedek. He uses this technique both in anticipation of his treatment of the Levitical priests and in reflecting on Ps. 110:4. The Levites were appointed to priesthood by virtue of their ancestry as descendants of Aaron. From the historical context of the Genesis passage we know that Melchizedek met Abraham long before God gave the guidelines for the old covenant priesthood. The lack of any reference to Melchizedek's parents or ancestors shows that considerations important for the Levites were not attached to Melchizedek's service as priest. Furthermore, the service of the Levites ended upon death, as the author points out in Hebrews 7:8, 23. Psalm

110:4, however, makes clear that Melchizedek holds his priesthood forever, a fact not contradicted by Genesis 14:17–20.

He collected a tenth from Abraham (7:6). The concept of the "tithe" was practiced across numerous societies of the ancient Mediterranean. Success in war or in one's profession could result in giving a tenth part to the gods. As with other places in Hebrews, however, the author draws on material for his discussion from the biblical text, specifically the laws concerning the tithe paid to the Levitical priests. In Numbers 18:20–32 the Lord instructs Aaron and Moses that the Levites, who would not receive a portion of the Promised Land as their inheritance, would receive the tithe from the rest of the Israelites as their inheritance in return for their work of serving in the Tent of Meeting. In turn, the Levites were to give as an offering to the Lord a tenth of what they received, the best and holiest part, as the Lord's portion.

The author's logic follows that the great patriarch Abraham, whose descendants, the Levites, would receive tithes from their fellow Israelites, gave a tithe to Melchizedek. This man was not a Levite, but Abraham tithed to him—and thus Levi, a future descendant of Abraham, who was still in Abraham's body, played a part in giving that tithe. This shows that Melchizedek was superior to the Levitical priests. It should be remembered that, in the case of the Levites, they were instructed to pay a tenth to the Lord through Aaron. They tithed to the Lord through a superior, who was the Lord's chief representative.

And blessed him who had the promises (7:6). As seen in the agricultural image of 6:7–8 the twin concepts of blessing and cursing are important motifs in the biblical literature. Individuals might bless God (e.g., Gen. 9:26; 14:20) or be blessed by God (e.g., Gen. 12:3; Num. 23:20). A blessing could be used informally as a greeting or in the event of a departure. Yet, a blessing could be a formal pronouncement of goodwill that was seen as having a positive impact on the blessed person's future. In the book of Genesis, the broader context for Melchizedek's meeting with Abram, the concept occurs over sixty times, many of the occurrences following the line of formal proclamations of goodwill.

The Superiority of Our Melchizedekan High Priest (7:11–28)

Now in inverse order the author probes two parts of God's "oath" in Psalm 110:4. Jesus as a priest "in the order of Melchizedek" constitutes the discussion of Hebrews 7:11–14, and the balance of the chapter concerns the phrase, "you are a priest forever." This section continues the author's use of *midrash* or running commentary on the Old Testament texts

BURNT OFFERINGS

A model of the courtyard of the tabernacle with the altar of burnt offering.

▼

(see comments on 7:1–10), but now the emphasis has shifted from the Genesis passage on Melchizedek to the Psalm passage.

For on the basis of it (7:11). In the NIV translation, "for on the basis of it the law was given to the people," the pronoun "it" seems to refer to the Levitical priesthood. Yet the translation might better be rendered "for concerning it" or "in the case of it." What the author has in mind are the directions given in the law concerning the establishment and function of the old covenant Levitical priesthood. During the time of the desert wanderings the Levites conducted worship in the tabernacle and took care of that structure (Num. 1:47–54; 3:14–39). The author points out that perfection was not attained through this priesthood.

There must also be a change of law (7:12). Insofar as Jesus has been appointed a priest apart from the normal guidelines for appointment detailed in the law, it is clear, in the author's view, that God has changed the law in some way. In other words, God has instituted a new basis for dealing with sin and sacrifice, as is also indicated by the change in covenant (8:7–13).

A different tribe (7:13). At the heart of this change in the law's requirement stands the primary basis for appointment as priest. In the old covenant system, appointment as priest was based on heredity—priests were taken from the tribe of Levi. That Jesus hailed from the tribe of Judah demonstrates this requirement has been set aside.

Our Lord descended from Judah (7:14). The tribe of Judah was, of course, one of the twelve tribes of the nation Israel, named for the sons of the man Israel. The man Judah was the one who interceded for his brother Joseph's life when his other brothers were about to kill him (Gen. 37:12–26) and then suggested they sell him into slavery instead (37:26–27). Significantly, his father's prophetic benediction concerning Judah included a statement about his descendants as rulers not only of the nation of Israel, but of the nations generally. This prophecy focused on a future ruler who would rule the nations: "The scepter will not depart from Judah, nor the ruler's staff from between his feet, until he comes to whom it belongs and the obedience of the nations is his" (49:10). The tribe of Judah historically was tied to the royal house of David, the archetypal ruler of God's people; in Revelation 5:5 Jesus is called the "Lion of the tribe of Judah, the Root of David."

The former regulation is set aside because it was weak and useless (7:18). Among the various first-century movements within Judaism, the view that certain aspects of past revelation have been overturned is seen especially in Christianity. The reason for this—illustrated preeminently by Hebrews—is that Christ, the Messiah, has become the reference point by which all of God's revelation should be understood. The author of Hebrews locates grounds in the Old Testament Scriptures for his assertion that the old covenant systems of priesthood and sacrifice have been superseded. According to Psalm 110:4 God has decided to appoint a priest by a means other than those found in the law.

The author goes on, however, to suggest the reason God "set aside" a regulation that, in the past, was binding. The old covenant law concerning appointment had its purpose in its time, but ultimately it was too weak and ineffective to accomplish the greater purposes of God. It was weak in that the priests of that system were mortal and limited by death, and the sacrifices were unable to cleanse permanently.

And it was not without an oath (7:20). The author alludes to the phrase in Psalm 110:4 that says, "The LORD has sworn and will not change his mind." No such oath can be found in relation to the Levitical priests. For the author of Hebrews this oath, made doubly strong by the assertion that the Lord will not change his mind, gives strong encouragement because it indicates a permanent provision for God's people.

Jesus has become the guarantee (7:22). Because God's oath must be seen as permanent, the threat of our change in status before God must be understood as having been dealt with decisively. Jesus has become the "guarantee" of a covenant that is "better." The word translated "guarantee" (*engyos*), which could also be

translated "guarantor," was common in legal contexts, but was not normally used in the ancient world to discuss covenants or testaments. In legal contexts the word indicated a person who guarantees the position or endeavors of another person by putting himself or herself at risk. In 7:22 the author pictures Jesus as the guarantee for God's covenant promises. As the originator of that covenant, through his sacrifice of himself, and his permanent position as the high priest of our new covenant with God, Jesus gives firm assurance that this relationship with God will last.

Such a high priest meets our need (7:26). The author now brings us back around to the place at which the section started in 5:1–3. In giving the general guidelines for high priesthood at the beginning of chapter 5, the author points out that the high priest under the old covenant served to meet the needs of God's people in a specific context. In that context, however, the high priest also had to deal with his own weaknesses. His sacrifices too had to be offered over and over again. Jesus, by contrast, has been appointed by different means (an oath) and has a superior basis for meeting our needs. He does not die and, thus, always lives to intercede for us. His sacrifice for sins was offered once for all. Therefore, he meets our needs in a superior way because he serves as the ever-present high priest whose sacrifice for sins does not need to be repeated.

A Key Transition (8:1–2)

With Hebrews 8 the author makes a major transition to the next great section of this book, a section dealing with Christ's superior sacrifice for sins. These

---

REFLECTIONS

THE PERMANENCE OF CHRIST'S priesthood and his ever-occurring intercession on our behalf should be causes of great peace and stability. This system of the new covenant, by definition, cannot be replaced with another system. Jesus is a priest "forever" and can save us completely. Therefore, we do not have to worry about our status before God. Jesus is the guarantee of covenant life lived in spiritual stability.

first two verses are a special form of transition that bridges the gap between two larger sections. Then 8:3–6 introduces the ministry of Christ as high priest and rivets our attention on the heavenly sphere of that ministry. This passage might be titled, "Introduction: The More Excellent Ministry of the Heavenly High Priest." The balance of the chapter (8:7–13) presents Jeremiah 31:31–34, the longest Old Testament quotation in the New Testament. By virtue of this quotation the author focuses attention on the superiority of the new covenant vis-à-vis the old covenant, using a rabbinic method of commentary by which the commentator draws out the implications of the passage.

One of the ways an ancient author could tie blocks of material together was by utilizing what have been called "hook words." In ancient Greek rhetoric this literary device was called *hysteron proteron*, literally "latter-former." The device "hooked" one literary unit to the next by presenting a key word (or words) used at the end of the first unit, at the beginning of the new unit. Thus a verbal bridge tied the two units together. The author of Hebrews does this by using the words "heavens" and "high priests" in Hebrews 7:26–28, words that correspond to "high priest" and "heaven" in 8:1. He also ties 8:1–2 to 8:4–6 by use of the word translated "high priest."

Who sat down at the right hand of the throne of the Majesty in heaven (8:1). The author has already drawn attention to Psalm 110:1 twice in the book, once with an allusion in Hebrews 1:3 and then with the quotation at 1:13. As with the allusion to that psalm verse in 1:3, the writer now adds to the words of the psalm the phrase "in heaven," which would have been understood as the location of the Son's exalted position at the "right hand."

The concept of "heaven" or "the heavens" meant different things to different philosophical and theological orientations of the first century world. Philo understood heaven more in Platonic

▶ The Heavenly Tabernacle in Judaism

A number of texts from the Dead Sea Scrolls speak of the new Jerusalem with a new temple (e.g., 2QNew Jerusalem; 5QNew Jerusalem). *Fourth Ezra*, a book from about 100 A.D. states, "For indeed the time will come, when the signs that I have foretold to you will come to pass, that the city that now is not seen shall appear, and the land that now is hidden shall be disclosed."[A-10] The "city that now is not seen" is the heavenly Jerusalem. In *Second Baruch*, from the first half of the second Christian century, the prophet looks into heaven and sees a vision of "the likeness of Zion, with its measurements, which was to be made after the likeness of the present sanctuary."[A-11] Finally, Wisdom of Solomon 9:8 states, "You have given command to build a temple on your holy mountain, and an altar in the city of your habitation, a copy of the holy tent that you prepared from the beginning." So the holy tent has been in heaven with God all along.

In Christian literature, Galatians 4:26 speaks of "the Jerusalem that is above," and Revelation 21:1–22:5, in describing the new heaven and new earth, describes the holy city, the new Jerusalem, coming down out of heaven. It is interesting that in this new city described in Revelation there is no temple building because "the Lord God Almighty and the Lamb are its temple."

terms as the sphere of the ideal reality. In the past the weight of scholarly opinion placed Hebrews in a philonic conceptual framework, but studies in the past forty years have taken a decided turn against this position. Most scholars on Hebrews are now convinced the author understands the concept of heaven in the tradition of first-century Jewish apocalyptic thought. In the Old Testament and post-biblical Judaism, heaven is seen as the dwelling place of God par excellence (e.g., 1 Kings 8:30–39). In the rabbinic literature specifically, heaven is the seat of God and is the focus of human prayer.[96]

The true tabernacle set up by the Lord, not by man (8:2). The tabernacle was the old covenant worship center where God met with his people (Ex. 25:1–27:21). It contained several items of importance, including the ark of the covenant, the table for the bread of the Presence, and the golden lampstand. In 25:9, 40 God tells Moses to make the tabernacle according to the pattern he would be shown on the mountain; this instruction lies behind an important theological vein of thought in early Judaism and early Christianity that held there were heavenly counterparts (either present or future) to the earthly Jerusalem and the earthly tabernacle or temple.

Introduction: The More Excellent Ministry of the Heavenly High Priest (8:3–13)

So it was necessary for this one also to have something to offer (8:3). In 5:1–10; 7:1–28, the author presented the appointment of the Son as a superior high priest. That section started with the statement, "Every high priest is selected from among men and is appointed to represent them in matters related to God, to offer gifts and sacrifices for sins" (5:1). Now the author provides a parallel introduction to the corresponding section running from 8:3 to 10:18, which deals with the superior high priest's heavenly offering: "Every high priest is appointed to offer both gifts and sacrifices, and so it was necessary for this one also to have something to offer."

Note that the proclamation of 5:1 places the statement concerning appointment before the statement concerning sacrifices for sins. This was done for emphasis, since the section beginning with 5:1 focuses on the Son's appointment to the office of high priest. At 8:3 the focus shifts to the necessity of a high priest having an offering to offer. This statement introduces the focus of 8:3–10:18: The Son, who has been appointed as a superior high priest (5:1–10; 7:1–28), has a superior, new covenant offering he has offered.

HIGH PRIEST

An artistic representation of the Jewish high priest in his vestments including the breastplate with twelve stones representing the tribes of Israel.

If he were on earth, he would not be a priest (8:4). The author alludes here to the argument he has made in 7:11–25. The earthly priesthood was one limited to tribal descent and limited by death. Psalm 110:4 shows that Christ is not a priest according to the earthly guidelines of the law. His priesthood involves rather a heavenly sacrifice offered in the heavenly sanctuary (Heb. 9:24).

A sanctuary that is a copy and shadow of what is in heaven (8:5). The word translated "copy" could be used variously to mean a sample, suggestion, symbol, outline, or example—something, in other words, that forms the basis for further instruction or imitation.[97] Thus, the word here means that Moses made the tabernacle as a sketch or shadow when compared to the real thing in heaven. The old covenant place of worship, as important as it was for that era, can only be conceived as an imperfect sketch of the heavenly reality, since human hands made it (cf. 9:11). As a "shadow" it imitates the heavenly original sufficiently to point to it. Yet as part of the earthly realm of existence, it is passing off the scene and ultimately is insufficient for the overarching purposes of God.

The time is coming, declares the Lord, when I will make a new covenant (8:8–13). Jeremiah 31:31–34 is part of a larger section of the prophetic book that has

▶ How the "New Covenant" Was Understood at Qumran

Among the Qumran sectarians, the "new covenant" passage from Jeremiah was interpreted to herald their eschatological community. Yet the contexts in which that community commented on the new covenant indicate a legalistic understanding of the covenant's implications:

But all those who have been brought into the covenant shall not enter the temple to kindle his altar in vain. . . . Unless they are careful to act in accordance with the exact interpretation of the law for the age of wickedness: to separate themselves from the sons of the pit; to abstain from wicked wealth which defiles, either by promise or by vow, and from the wealth of the temple and from stealing from the poor of the people, from making their widows their spoils and from murdering orphans; to separate unclean from clean and differentiate between the holy and the common; to keep the Sabbath day according to the exact interpretation, and the festivals and the day of fasting, according to what they had discovered, those who entered the new covenant in the land of Damascus. . . . (CD 6:11b–19)

For the earliest Christians the implications of the new covenant were very different from those drawn by Jews at Qumran. Rather than a legalistic approach that focuses on a believer's shortcomings in relation to the covenant, the early Christians understood the covenant to be a proclamation of God's grace brought through the sacrificial death of Christ and celebrated in the Lord's Supper (Luke 22:20; 1 Cor. 11:25). The new covenant does not have to do with a legalistic approach to the law, the letter that kills, but is a covenant of the life-giving Spirit (2 Cor. 3:6).

The author of Hebrews does not provide a detailed commentary on aspects of the Jeremiah passage. It might be argued that the primary characteristics of the covenant are self-evident when one simply reads the passage. The covenant involves the laws of God internalized, placed in the minds and written on the hearts of God's people. In truth God will be their God (they will not bow before idols), and each and every one will know God. Finally, the new covenant involves forgiveness from sins.

◀

THE TABERNACLE

A model of the tabernacle and its courtyard.

been titled "The Book of Consolation" (30:1–33:26). Whereas the earlier chapters of Jeremiah focus on judgment, these chapters offer hope for the future of God's people.[98]

By calling this covenant "new" (8:13). In 8:13 one encounters a rabbinic technique of commentary used to bring into focus a key reason the author has quoted the passage from Jeremiah at this point in the book. Rabbis sometimes quoted a text

and then commented on the implications of a single word or phrase. The author of Hebrews focuses attention on the word "new" in the Jeremiah passage. He stresses that the designation "new" covenant means there was an "old" covenant that is now obsolete. His greater purpose is to show that the new covenant established by the heavenly, Day of Atonement sacrifice of Christ has been proclaimed superior to the old covenant in which the levitical priests were involved.

The Old Covenant Structure and Regulations for Worship (9:1–10)

In 9:1–10:18 the author addresses the specific ways in which Christ's new covenant ministry of sacrifice should be seen as superior to the sacrificial ministry of the priests under the old covenant. In order to highlight the contrasts, he begins by explaining aspects of the worship

◀ *left*

THE ARK OF THE COVENANT

A bas-relief of the ark from the synagogue at Capernaum.

under the old covenant in 9:1–10. Three characteristics form the focus of attention: (1) the *place* of the offerings in the earthly tabernacle (9:1–6); (2) the *blood* of the offerings (9:7); and (3) the perpetual *nature* of the offerings (9:6–7, 9–10). Then in 9:11–10:18 he shows how Christ's sacrifice is superior at every turn: (1) the *place* of his offering was in heaven rather than on earth (9:11, 23–25; 10:12–13); (2) the *blood* of the offering was Christ's own rather than the blood of mere animals (9:12–28); and (3) the offering of Christ was *eternally* effective, eradicating a need for continual offerings (9:25–26; 10:1–18).

THE TABERNACLE

A life-size model set up in the Timnah.

▼

Regulations for worship (9:1). The word translated "regulations" refers to requirements or commandments and is related to a whole family of Greek words associated with the concept of justice or righteousness. What the author has in mind are those guidelines, "God's just directives," concerning how the sacrificial worship practices were to be conducted by the priests under the old covenant. These regulations are explained in 9:6–7.

In its first room were the lampstand, the table and the consecrated bread (9:2). Being especially concerned with movement of the priests and high priest into the tabernacle, the author of Hebrews explains that there was a "first" or outer room called the Holy Place (9:2) and an "inner" room designated the "Most Holy Place" (9:3). These two rooms were separated by a curtain, behind which only the high priest could go once per year, on the Day of Atonement.

The lampstand, made of pure gold, had six flowered branches protruding from its sides, three to a side. There were

▶ The Tabernacle

The tabernacle was the tent, or moveable worship center, erected under the leadership of Moses during the desert wanderings. The Hebrew term we render as "tabernacle" relates to the concept of dwelling, and it was the physical structure identified with the presence of God. The structure also was called the "sanctuary," the "tent of meeting" (e.g., Ex. 33:7; Num. 11:16), simply "the tent," and "the tabernacle of the testimony" (Ex. 38:21), among other designations. The instructions concerning the building of the tabernacle are found in Exodus 25–31; 35–40. Gifts freely given by the Israelites were to supply the materials needed for construction—among them gold, silver, bronze,

fine linen, yarn colored blue, purple, and scarlet, goat hair, ram skins dyed red and sea cow hides, and acacia wood (25:1–5).

In structure the tabernacle was a tent made up of a series of curtains. Ten curtains, all the same size, made from the finely twisted linen, formed the inner part of the tabernacle (Ex. 26:1–2), which was covered with eleven curtains of goat hair (26:7–13), which in turn were covered with red ram skins and the hides of sea cows (26:14). All of these curtains were supported by frames made of acacia wood, overlaid with gold, and by various kinds of clasps and loops (26:15–29).

seven lamps on the stand, and the lampstand was situated on the south side of the Holy Place (Ex. 25:31–40; 26:35). Also called the *menorah* (a Hebrew word) in Jewish history, the lampstand was the most popular image in ancient Jewish art, appearing on coins, ceramic lamps, and the walls of synagogues and tombs. The earliest known picture of the lampstand occurs on a coin from the reign of Antigonus Mattathias (40–37 B.C.).[99]

The table for the bread of the Presence, like the frames of the tabernacle, was made of acacia wood overlaid with gold. It was two cubits long, a cubit wide, and one and a half cubits high (Ex. 25:23–30). It is difficult to determine the exact measurements by today's reckoning, since a "cubit" varied between seventeen and twenty-one inches and had its basis in the distance between a person's elbow and the tip of the middle finger.[100] The four corners of the table had four gold rings through which acacia poles were placed to carry the table. In addition, the plates and utensils for the table were also made of pure gold. The consecrated bread, called the "showbread" or "bread of the Presence," consisted of

twelve loaves of unleavened bread that symbolized God's covenant with the Israelites. These were arranged on the table in two rows of six loaves, and were to be eaten only by Aaron and his sons (Lev. 24:5–9). The table itself was consecrated by sacred oil and placed on the north side of the Holy Place (Ex. 26:35).

Behind the second curtain was a room called the Most Holy Place (9:3). Two curtains, or veils, served as sacred barriers for the tabernacle. The first served as the covering for the entrance to the tent. This curtain was made of "blue, purple and scarlet yarn and finely twisted linen." Five posts, made of acacia wood and overlaid with gold, held up the curtain, and bronze bases stabilized these posts (Ex. 26:36–37).

The second and more significant curtain separated the outer room from the inner—the "Most Holy Place." This second curtain also was made of "blue, purple and scarlet yarn and finely twisted linen," but Exodus adds that a skilled craftsman embroidered cherubim on the curtain. Gold hooks were attached to four acacia posts overlaid with gold, and the posts sat on silver bases (rather than

ITEMS FROM THE HOLY PLACE

(left) A model of the golden table of showbread with two stacks of bread and two golden bowls of incense.

(right) The golden lampstand *(menorah)*.
▼

bases of bronze as with the first curtain) (Ex. 26:31–32).

In various strands of Jewish interpretation in the ancient world the curtain separating the Holy Place from the Most Holy Place was understood as symbolic of various realities. For instance, the veil could be understood as symbolic of the separation of heaven and earth, or perhaps two parts of heaven. Regardless, the key point for all interpretations focused on the veil as a separator from the presence of God.[101] For the author of Hebrews the "second curtain" is that through which the high priest passed into that presence. Christ as high priest takes the new covenant believer with him through the curtain into the very presence of God (Heb. 10:19–20).

The golden altar of incense (9:4). The golden altar of incense was another item of the tabernacle made of acacia wood and overlaid with gold. The altar was a cubit long and a cubit wide, standing two cubits high. Like the table for the consecrated bread, the altar had rings through which poles of acacia wood could be placed for carrying it. The purpose of the altar, as its name suggests, was to burn incense before the Lord. Aaron was instructed to burn incense on the altar every morning and every evening at twi-

light, both times corresponding to his tending of the lamps in the tabernacle. Significantly, the altar of incense also played a role in the Day of Atonement ritual. Blood from the atoning sin offering was to be placed on the horns of the altar (Ex. 30:1–10).

Hebrews places the altar of incense in the Most Holy Place, yet in the Old Testament and in the history of interpretation, the location of the altar is ambiguous. However, the altar is closely associated with the ark in many Old Testament passages.

The gold-covered ark of the covenant (9:4). The ark of the covenant has numerous designations in the Old Testament, among them, "the ark," "the ark of God," "the ark of the testimony," and "the ark of the Lord." It was the most important item of furniture in the tabernacle since it represented the presence of God. The ark was a chest made of acacia wood and overlaid with gold both inside and out. The chest was two and a half cubits long, one and a half cubits wide, and one and a half cubits high; it had four gold rings through which acacia poles would be placed for carrying it. The cover for the ark was made of pure gold and had a golden cherub on each end, the two facing each other, with their wings spread upward (Ex. 25:10–22). The "testimony" (i.e., the tablets of the Ten Commandments) was placed in the ark. In all of ancient literature, Hebrews alone adds that the jar of manna and Aaron's staff were also in the ark.

The manna was from God's provision of food for the desert wanderers recounted in Exodus 16. The jar of manna was kept as a memorial for future generations, Aaron placing the jar in front of the ark (16:34). Numbers 17 provides the

ALTAR OF INCENSE

▼

◄

THE ARK OF THE COVENANT AND ITS CONTENTS

A model of the ark, Aaron's rod, the two stone tablets, and the golden pot of manna.

account of Aaron's staff budding. In response to rebellion against the leadership of Moses and Aaron, God had Moses gather twelve staffs, one to represent the leader of each of the twelve tribes. These staffs were placed in the Tent of Meeting for God to single out his chosen leader. Aaron's staff evidenced God's choice by budding, blossoming, and producing almonds. The Lord then instructed Moses to put Aaron's staff back in front of the Testimony as a reminder to those who would rebel against the Lord's chosen leaders (17:1–13).

The cherubim of the Glory (9:5). Rather than human in form, the cherubim are winged angels of composite animal form, sometimes having human characteristics as well, being one category of angels found in the Old Testament and extrabiblical, Jewish literature.[102] The designation "cherubim" may be derived from a word meaning "intercessor," and in the biblical witness, these angelic beings are associated especially with the presence of God. They guard the tree of life (Gen. 3:24), flank God's throne (Ps. 80:1; 99:1;

Isa. 37:16), and carry Yahweh through the heavens (Ps. 18:10). Images of cherubim were crafted as part of the ark's cover and were embroidered on the curtain leading into the Most Holy Place (Ex. 25:18–20; 26:31–32).

REFLECTIONS

THE DETAILS OF THE OLD COVENANT WORSHIP EXPE-riences related to the tabernacle must seem tedious and monotonous to most modern readers. Yet, we should not miss key points of the Christian faith to which they speak. First, God is a holy God from whom people are separated because of sin. The "sacred barrier" of the Holy Place, the necessity of sacrifices, and the unapproachable nature of the Most Holy Place all speak to humanity's foundational problem in relation to God. Yet, and this is a second key point, God's initiative in the construction of the tabernacle whispers his desire for more in relation to us. He wants to be approached; he wants to relate to his people. While the existence of the Holy Place shows that the way into God's presence for his people had not yet been revealed, the sacrifices and high priesthood demonstrate God's desire that sin not have the final word. The sacrifice and high priesthood of Jesus gave the ultimate answer to the problem and to God's desire that we come near to him.

The Tabernacle

A portable temple for the wilderness journey

The new religious observances taught by Moses in the desert centered on rituals connected with the tabernacle, and amplified Israel's sense of separateness, purity, and oneness under the Lordship of Yahweh.

A few desert shrines have been found in Sinai, notably at Serabit el-Khadem and at Timnah in the Negev, and show marked Egyptian influence.

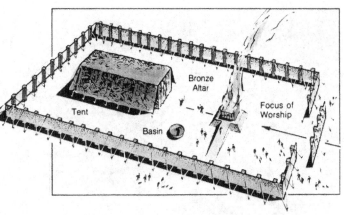

Bronze Altar

Tent

Basin

Focus of Worship

Hides of Sea Cows, providing a waterproof covering and "camouflaging" the rich interior from enemies and bandits

Ram skins, Dyed Red

Goat hair

Fine twisted linen, blue, purple, and scarlet yarn, yarn with cherubim embroidered by skilled craftsmen.

Specific cultural antecedents to portable shrines carried on poles and covered with thin sheets of gold can be found in ancient Egypt as early as the Old Kingdom (2800–2250 B.C.), but were especially prominent in the 18th and 19th dynasties (1570–1180). The best examples come from the fabulous tomb of Tutankhamun, c. 1350.

Comparisons of construction in the text of Ex. 25–40 with the frames, shrines, poles, sheathing, draped fabric covers, gilt rosettes, and winged protective figures from the shrine of Tutankhamun are instructive. The period, the Late Bronze Age, is equivalent in all dating systems to the era of Moses and the Exodus.

Most Holy Place

Table with Bread of Presence

Holy Place

Ark of the Covenant

Posts—acacia wood overlaid with gold, gold tops and silver bases

Veil

Incense Altar

Crossbars

Lampstand

Upright frames—acacia wood overlaid with gold

Silver bases

© Hugh Claycombe 1997

The priests entered regularly into the outer room (9:6). Ministry in the Holy Place, the outer room of the tabernacle, was the priests' responsibility. They entered to keep the lamps lit and to change the bread of the Presence (Ex. 27:20–21; Lev. 24:8).

But only the high priest entered the inner room (9:7). The Day of Atonement sacrifice, offered on the tenth day of the seventh month (September/October), was the most important sacrifice of the year for the Israelites. This sacrifice covered all of the sins not covered in the previous year by other sacrifices. On this one day of the year the people drew near to God by the high priest's entering the Most Holy Place with the Day of Atonement sacrifice (Lev. 16:1–25). Two animals were sacrificed in the ceremony, a bull as a sin offering for Aaron and his household, and a goat for the sins of the people. The blood of these two animals was sprinkled in the Most Holy Place (16:11–17).

The first tabernacle was still standing (9:8). The phrase rendered "first tabernacle" by the NIV is a reference to the outer room of the old covenant tabernacle. The author's point here is that the existence of the Holy Place, a sacred space separating God's people from his presence in the Most Holy Place, was indicative of the old covenant era. The way into that presence for his people in general had not yet been revealed.

Christ's Superior Ministry As Priest (9:11–28)

The greater and more perfect tabernacle (9:11). As with 8:2, the author understands that there exists a heavenly tabernacle in the heavenly city of God (cf. 12:22), a

▶ The Jerusalem Temple

What about the Jerusalem temple? Given that the temple in Jerusalem was at the very center of Jewish life until its destruction in A.D. 70, it is reasonable to ask why the author of Hebrews focuses on the Old Testament tabernacle rather than the first-century temple. The question is especially pertinent if, as argued in our introduction, Hebrews was written in the 60s just prior to the Jewish war with Rome, when the temple was still a glorious symbol of contemporary Judaism. Would not the author have found in the temple a ready target for his statements concerning the ineffectual nature of the older covenant? Indeed, some commentators have suggested that the uses of the present tense to speak of old covenant worship activity are an indication that the contemporary temple activities were in mind and demonstrate that the temple in Jerusalem was still standing when Hebrews was written. However,

this argument falters upon further research, for texts such as Josephus' *Antiquities, 1 Clement* 31:2, and *Barnabas* 7–8, all of which were written after the destruction of the Jerusalem temple, similarly speak of old covenant worship in the present tense.[A-12]

There probably are two main, interrelated reasons why the author focuses on the tabernacle rather than the temple. First, he is interested in the dynamics surrounding the establishment of the old covenant (see esp. 8:4–6; 9:18–22), so he can contrast it with the establishment of the new covenant sacrifice of Christ. Second, the author grounds his entire sermon in the Old Testament Scriptures. He is interested in demonstrating the superiority of Christ's new covenant from the authoritative Word of God, and it is the tabernacle, not the temple of the first century, to which the Scriptures bear witness.

concept common in Jewish apocalyptic of his era. The writers of Qumran, *4 Ezra, 2 Baruch*, and Wisdom of Solomon, for instance, all mention the heavenly Jerusalem with its heavenly place of worship.

The blood of goats and calves (9:12). Leviticus 16 gives the details of the Day of Atonement sacrifices, which included the sacrifice of a goat and a young bull (Lev. 16:6–10). As with the broader context, this specific sacrifice is in view here.

The ashes of a heifer sprinkled (9:13). In Numbers 19 we find instructions concerning the "red heifer." The Israelites were commanded to bring Moses and Aaron a perfect heifer that had never been under a yoke. It was taken outside the camp and killed, and its blood was sprinkled seven times toward the front of the Tent of Meeting. The animal was burned then and its ashes collected for ceremonial cleansing. These ashes could be mixed with water and sprinkled on an unclean person. The tabernacle also had to be sprinkled when an Israelite had

GOATS

▼

defiled the worship center by touching a dead body (Num. 19:1–21).

Cleanse our consciences (9:14). The term translated as "conscience(s)" in 9:9, 14 was used rarely in Greek literature prior to 200 B.C., but is found in first-century A.D. writers such as Plutarch, Philo, and Josephus. In A.D 59 a papyrus tells of a former soldier named Lucius Pamiseus, who met a procession of donkeys carrying stones and led by a slave. Lucius suffered a violent kick by one of the donkeys, and the frightened slave, because of his bad "conscience," ran away.[103] The term connotes a personal knowledge of something, or more specifically, the moral "consciousness" of good and evil. The problem with the old covenant system of sacrifice was its inability to deal with a worshiper's awareness of personal guilt.

Christ is the mediator (9:15). The word translated "mediator" was used widely in the Greco-Roman period, often with legal overtones. It was used for an arbiter in a political dispute or to one who settled an argument over a business deal. It also connoted a "guarantor" of an oath given in a legal situation. In religious contexts the word referred to someone who represented the people before God. Philo calls both Moses and angels mediators between God and his people.[104] In the New Testament, Jesus is the supreme mediator between God and people (1 Tim. 2:5; Heb. 8:6; 12:24).

He has died as a ransom to set them free (9:15). The word rendered "ransom" by the NIV does not occur often outside the New Testament, and then found especially in Paul's letters. It refers to the liberation effected by God on behalf of his people, by his dealing with sin (Rom. 3:24; 1 Cor. 1:30).

In the case of a will, it is necessary to prove the death (9:16). The translation of the Greek term *diathēkē* here as "will" is out of step with the context, which has to do with the ratification of a covenant. In the context the author is concerned with the establishment of the older covenant through sacrifice (9:12–14, 18–22). The sense of 9:16–17 is that the covenant was established by a death. In the death of the sacrificial animal the ratifier's death was symbolically realized. Such a death is necessary for the establishment of the covenant.

Blood (9:18). For the past century at least, commentators have misunderstood the blood motif in the New Testament to represent "life."[105] Instead, the concept of blood in the Scriptures represents death. In Hebrews specifically the author, when referring to the shedding of Christ's blood, is speaking of his sacrificial death

that effects our cleansing (9:14), brings us freedom (9:15), and establishes the new covenant.

He took the blood of calves, together with water, scarlet wool and . . . hyssop (9:19). Exodus 24:8 recounts that Moses ratified the first covenant between God and his people by the sprinkling of blood: "Moses then took the blood, sprinkled it on the people and said, 'This is the blood of the covenant that the LORD has made with you in accordance with all these words.'"

He sprinkled with the blood both the tabernacle and everything used in its ceremonies (9:21). The assertion that Moses sprinkled the tabernacle and vessels used in worship may seem problematic, since Exodus does not tell us this. Yet, often interpreters of the ancient world, by verbal analogy, considered related passages of Scripture, with similar language, together. For instance, the Day of Atonement ritual in Leviticus 16 and the ceremony of the

◀

SACRIFICE AT THE
TABERNACLE

red heifer in Numbers 19 both involved sprinkling the Tent of Meeting (Num. 19:4; Lev. 16:14–19), and the former also included sprinkling of the altar and the cover of the ark.

But the heavenly things themselves [purified] with better sacrifices (9:23). Why would the heavenly things need to be purified? The answer is found in the instructions concerning the Day of Atonement sacrifice:

> In this way he will make atonement for the Most Holy Place because of *the uncleanness and rebellion of the Israelites*, whatever their sins have been. He is to do the same for the Tent of Meeting, which is among them *in the midst of their uncleanness*. No one is to be in the Tent of Meeting from the time Aaron goes in to make atonement in the Most Holy Place until he comes out, having made atonement for himself, his household and the whole community of Israel.
>
> Then he shall come out to the altar that is before the LORD and make atonement for it. He shall take some of the bull's blood and some of the goat's blood and put it on all the horns of the altar. He shall sprinkle some of the blood on it with his finger seven times *to cleanse it and to consecrate it from the uncleanness of the Israelites* (Lev. 16:16–19; italics added).

In other words, the need for cleansing the earthly worship center and its furniture had nothing to do with the uncleanness of the center or its furniture, but rather related to the uncleanness of the people. Therefore, the "heavenly things" would need to be cleansed, in the author's conception, for the same reason.

To bring salvation (9:28). In secular Greek the word translated "salvation" speaks of deliverance from a perilous situation, such as war, an enemy, a storm, or a difficult trip. In a medical context it speaks of good health. The New Testament also uses the word for such secular meanings, but the theological sense predominates. Salvation is deliverance from sin and God's coming wrath (Luke 1:68; Rom. 5:9), and it may be seen as already experienced (Rom. 8:24), a continuing process (1 Cor. 1:18), and a reality consummated in the future, as here in Hebrews 9:28.[106]

The Provisional Nature of the Old Covenant Worship Laws (10:1–18)

Hebrews 10:1–18 serves as the crowning point in the author's treatment of Christ's superior appointment as a high priest, who offers a superior offering. In 9:11–28 the focus has been on the offering's superiority based on (1) Christ's blood being superior to the blood of the Day of Atonement sacrifices, and (2) its location in the heavenly tabernacle. The author now focuses attention on a third point in favor of the Son's offering as superior: It was made just one time, which was sufficient for the permanent cleansing of God's people.

A shadow (10:1). In 8:5 the author makes the point that the tabernacle was a "shadow" of God's heavenly dwelling, merely mimicking the greater reality. He now points out that the law, providing instructions for approaching God through animal sacrifices in an earthly tent, is of the same nature, being only the "shadow . . . not the realities themselves." The word rendered "shadow" also can be translated as a "foreshadowing," a "sketch," or a "faint outline." The point is that it does not embody the greater reality of which it hints. In Plato's allegory of the cave the philosopher also contrasts the shadows from the images casting the shadows.[107] Cicero used the imagery to contrast natural and civil law, suggesting that humans do not possess a firm and clear model of true law and real justice, but rather utilize a shadow of the real thing.[108] Harold Attridge rightly notes that Hebrews uses Platonic terms, but applies them to a horizontal or temporal relationship between two time periods.[109] Those things of the past are mere shadows of the greater realities that have now been manifested. In Colossians 2:16–17 Paul uses a phrase similar to "a shadow of the good things that are coming," found here in Hebrews 10:1:

> Therefore do not let anyone judge you by what you eat or drink, or with regard to a religious festival, a New Moon celebration or a Sabbath day. These are a shadow of the things that were to come; the reality, however, is found in Christ.

Reminder of sin (10:3). In Numbers 5:15 the offering for a woman suspected of adultery is called "a reminder offering." The man who suspected his wife of adultery, with his wife, was to take an offering of barley flour to the priest. The priest mixed holy water and dust from the floor of the tabernacle, and if the woman was guilty and drank the mixture of water and dust, while holding in her hands the grain offering, it was a curse to her, causing tremendous suffering. The point is that the barley offering was a reminder of sin that brought sin to light. Commenting on this passage from Num-

bers, Philo remarks that God does not take delight in the sacrifices of people who are not virtuous. If a group of persons has a blazing altar fire that is not accompanied by good hearts, those persons' sacrifices only remind God of their ignorance and sinfulness.

Hebrews' point applies to the whole of the old covenant sacrificial system, as it is epitomized in the Day of Atonement sacrifice. Since the sacrifices really cannot cleanse the worshipers, as is shown by the offerings' repetition, all they really serve to do is affirm the perpetual state of sin in which the worshipers suffer. The offerings, thus, in their inability to remove sin, remind of sin.

"Sacrifice and offering you did not desire" [Ps. 40:6–8] (10:5–10). Psalm 40, a psalm of David, falls roughly into two movements, the first (40:1–11) praising God for his good gifts and proclaiming the psalmist's desire to do God's will, and the second (40:12–17) seeking God's help in a time of great need. Our author focuses on two points from the first half of the psalm that together convey the message that submission to God's will is more important than the offering of sacrifices. First, he highlights the

ANIMALS APPOINTED FOR SACRIFICE
▼

proclamation of God: "Sacrifice and offering you did not desire," and the parallel, "with burnt offerings and sin offerings you were not pleased." Tucked between these parallel statements is the statement, "but a body you prepared for me." Hebrews takes this statement from the LXX. The Hebrew behind the Greek text reads obscurely, "you have dug ears for me," perhaps meaning that God has prepared the psalmist's body for a posture of obedience, ready to hear and obey God's command. The main point concerning sacrifices, however, fits the broader context in which the author shows that God ultimately is not interested in sacrifices as an end in themselves.

The second part of the quotation finds the psalmist quoting himself, "Here I am—it is written about me in the scroll—I have come to do your will, O God." Prior to about the second century A.D. books existed in the scroll form. Sheets of papyrus or other materials, such as leather or even metal, were attached end on end and rolled up in a scroll. The scroll spoken of here may have originally been the laws of God concerning the king. For the author of Hebrews, who takes the psalm as Christological, the scroll probably speaks of the whole witness of the Scriptures. Nevertheless, the psalm confesses a willingness to do the will of God.

In interpreting the psalm Christologically, Hebrews takes the order of the material in this section as significant. The first part concerning sacrifices and offerings, for the author, alludes to the sacrificial system of the old covenant. The fact that Christ, through the Old Testament Scripture, follows with "Then I said, 'Here I am . . . I have come to do your will,'" demonstrates that there is a temporal sequence to the psalm, showing that "he sets aside the first to establish the second" (10:9). In fine rabbinic style, the author interprets the "then" in the text as indicative of that sequence. The words translated "sets aside" and "establish" in 10:9 are legal terms from the era for

A SCROLL

The "Temple Scroll" from Qumran.

annulment and institution. Christ's willingness to submit obediently to his Father's will and to be a sacrifice for sins has legally annulled the old covenant sacrificial system and instituted the new covenant of Jeremiah 31. So, "by that will, we have been made holy through the sacrifice of the body of Jesus Christ once for all" (Heb. 10:10).

But when this priest had offered for all time one sacrifice for sins (10:12). Rhetorical arguments often used contrasts to show the relative strengths and weaknesses of various positions, people, or institutions. Here the author highlights four comparisons between the old and new covenant offerings. First, the old covenant offerings were presented daily, whereas Christ's offering was made but once. Second, the priests stood when presenting their offerings, but Christ's offering climaxed in his sitting down at the right hand of God. Third, under the old covenant system numerous sacrifices were made, whereas Christ made but one. Finally, the old covenant offerings could never take away sins, but Christ's sacrifice has accomplished that feat for those for whom the sacrifice was offered.

Hebrews 10:12 alludes to Psalm 110:1, the fourth reference to that verse in this book (see comments on Heb. 1:3). As used here in 10:12 the psalm verse emphasizes the finality and decisive nature of Christ's sacrifice for sins. For Hebrews, that the Son has sat down in his place of authority until the end of the age when all his enemies will be dealt their final blow shows that his sacrifice was completely sufficient for the forgiveness of sins. He is not a priest who must stand time and again to offer ineffectual sacrifices. His one sacrifice is enough. The new covenant people have

been made whole, complete, and perfectly suited for entrance into the presence of the Father.

"This is the covenant I will make with them" [Jer. 31:33–34] (10:15–18). The author now quotes a portion of Jeremiah 31:31–34, which he quoted in full at Hebrews 8:8–12. The quotation here, which highlights parts of Jeremiah 31:33–34, has two purposes, one literary and the other theological. Literarily, the quotation works with the longer quotation of the same passage in chapter 8 to form brackets around this section of Hebrews dealing with Christ's new covenant offering. The use of same or similar material at the beginning and ending of a section was called an *inclusio* and functions somewhat like paragraph or section headings function today, marking larger sections of a text or discourse. Theologically the author understands Jeremiah 31 to affirm what he has been arguing since chapter 8. Sin has been completely forgiven because of the decisive, new covenant sacrifice of Christ. This fact is in the warp and woof

R E F L E C T I O N S

THE BOOK OF HEBREWS DEALS EXTENSIVELY WITH how decisively the Son of God has dealt with our sin. His one sacrifice has provided complete forgiveness for all our sins for all time. Since we continue to deal with sin—alas, it still is a power against which we struggle—it is easy to forget the decisiveness with which our sin has been addressed. Hebrews proclaims that new covenant believers no longer have a "consciousness of sin," meaning an awareness of sin as prohibitive of our relationship with God. Rather, we have free entrance into the Most Holy Place by virtue of our high priest, Jesus. This is a cause for great celebration. Our sins past and present have already been paid for by one sacrifice, a sacrifice so effective that it never needs to be repeated.

of the new covenant. To be a person of the new covenant is to be a person completely forgiven.

Where these have been forgiven, there is no longer any sacrifice for sin (10:18). A rabbi at times would quote a passage and then state an obvious implication of that quotation, as the author does here. Since Christ has made a once-for-all sacrifice, every system of sacrifice has been outdated or annulled. Sacrifice for sin has been rendered a thing of the past.

Strong Encouragement for Christian Commitment (10:19–25)

Hebrews 10:19–25 forms the closing of an *inclusio* that the author started at 4:14–16. In this case the author marks the great central section on the Son's appointment to (5:1–10; 7:1–28) and ministry as a superior high priest (8:3–10:18) by including no fewer than eight parallel elements in 4:14–16 and 10:19–25.[110] Packed in these five verses we find the main points of the author's message. We have a superior basis for drawing near to God and holding fast to our confession, namely, our new covenant relationship with Jesus, the Son of God, who functions as our great high priest.

Since we have confidence (10:19). A rare word in ancient Greek literature, the word translated "confidence" connotes a freedom of expression and openness of conduct.[111] In ancient Jewish thought the concept relates at points to approaching God in prayer. Therefore, on the basis of Jesus' ministry as our high priest, we have courage, a reasonable boldness to approach God in his heavenly Most Holy Place.

A new and living way opened for us through the curtain (10:20). The imagery of 10:20 has its basis in the Day of Atonement ritual of the older covenant. Christ not only passes through the curtain as our high priest, but blazes a trail for us to follow. That this way is "new" may mean that it was previously unavailable, and its description as "living" suggests that we take it by association with the Living One.

In Greek and Roman heroic traditions, of which the author of Hebrews certainly was aware, the champion of the trail, someone who paved the way for others at great personal sacrifice, constituted an important theme. For instance, in the *Epitome* (1.14.3) of Lucius Annaeus Florus one finds this comment on the valor of the consul Decius Mus:

> . . . while the other consul, as though acting upon a warning from heaven, with veiled head devoted himself to the infernal gods in front of the army, in order that, by hurling himself where the enemy's weapons

right ▶

THE CURTAIN

A representation of the Most Holy Place with a priest before the Ark of the Covenant.

were thickest, he *might open up a new path to victory along the track of his own lifeblood.*[112]

Having our hearts sprinkled . . . and having our bodies washed with pure water (10:22). Commentators often have found in the references to sprinkling and washing in 10:22 references to Christian baptism. However, the backdrop of the old covenant purification rituals is in play here. The author has already referred to those rituals, for example, in 9:13–14, where they parallel Christ's cleansing of our consciences, and 9:19–23, where they occur in the inauguration of covenants. Our hearts are sprinkled and our bodies washed by the sacrifice of Christ.

Love and good deeds (10:24). To "spur . . . on" translates a noun that can be used either positively, in the sense of encouragement, or negatively with the meaning "irritation" or "sharp disagreement" (cf. Acts 15:39, where Paul and Barnabas had such a conflict). Here it is used positively. Christians are to relate to one another in such a way that encouragement in love and good deeds results. Authentic Christian love expresses itself in good works, and the challenge to such a love forms a cornerstone of a basic Christian ethic.[113]

The Day approaching (10:25). Old Testament prophets spoke of a "day" or "days" that would result in judgment for the Lord's enemies and redemption for his people.[114] The Israelites of Amos's day called for the day of the Lord, expecting it to be a day of light; but the prophet warned that for them, the unrighteous, it would be a day of darkness (Amos 5:18). In apocalyptic literature, the day often is called the "day of judgment."[115] "The Day"

for Hebrews, and the New Testament generally, is the day of Christ's return.[116]

Further Warnings and Encouragement (10:26–39)

These verses may be divided into two main movements. The first constitutes a harsh warning—perhaps the harshest in the book (10:26–31). The author crafts this warning around a technique used both among the rabbis and the rhetoricians of the day. This technique, "an argument from lesser to greater," suggests that if something is true in a lesser situation, it is more certainly true in a greater situation and normally carries greater implications. The author of Hebrews argues that if those who rejected the law of Moses died without mercy upon the testimony of two or three witnesses, those who have trampled the Son of God under foot, treated the blood of the covenant as unholy, and insulted the Spirit of grace deserve an even greater punishment. The second movement hands out encouragement in large doses, especially by instructing the readers to remember their past faithfulness (10:32–39). This pattern of harsh warning followed by a softened word of encouragement is found also at 6:4–12.

Deliberately keep on sinning (10:26). The Old Testament addresses what is called "sinning with a high hand," a rebellion against the laws of the Lord that was considered equivalent to blasphemy. Note Numbers 15:30–31: "But anyone who sins defiantly, whether native-born or alien, blasphemes the LORD, and that person must be cut off from his people. Because he has despised the LORD's word and broken his commands, that person must surely be cut off . . . his guilt remains on him." In Hebrews 10:26 the person who remains in a state of rebellion after receiving a knowledge of the gospel has nowhere else to go for forgiveness. "No sacrifice for sins is left" because Jesus has annulled all other sacrifices as a means of dealing with sin and relating to God.

Raging fire that will consume the enemies of God (10:27). An allusion to Isaiah 26:10–11, this fire constitutes a judgment of the wicked and a vindication of those who truly are God's people:

> Though grace is shown to the wicked,
>   they do not learn righteousness;
> even in a land of uprightness they go
>   on doing evil
>   and regard not the majesty of the
>   LORD.
> O LORD, your hand is lifted high,
>   but they do not see it.
> Let them see your zeal for your people
>   and be put to shame;
>   let the fire reserved for your
>   enemies consume them.

The wicked will be put to shame, God's fire consuming them.

Anyone who rejected the law of Moses died without mercy (10:28). Deuteronomy 17:2–7 commands that those who violate God's covenant by worshiping other gods must be put to death by stoning. This is only done if there is more than one witness to the breaking of the covenant, and the witnesses are to cast the first stones. According to Deuteronomy 13:8 the worshiper of false gods is to be stoned without mercy.

Trampled the Son of God under foot, who has treated as an unholy thing the blood of the covenant (10:29). To reject

the new covenant high priest, Jesus, and his offering for sin is a greater travesty than those who turned to other gods under the old covenant. The image of trampling someone under foot was used both in classical literature and the Old Testament as an image of utter contempt. Further, those familiar with the ceremonial laws of sacrifice knew the requirements for a fit offering. The word translated as "unholy" means common, defiled, or unclean; in the context of the Levitical purity laws of the LXX, it referred to that which was ceremonially impure, not worthy of sacrifice to God. Thus, those who have rejected Christ have considered his sacrifice as unworthy, unclean, or inappropriate as an offering for sin.

For we know him who said (10:30). The seriousness of the situation for those who have turned away from Christ finds further expression with words from the Song of Moses in Deuteronomy 32. This eloquent song, offered by the lawgiver at the end of his life, speaks of God's judgment toward a faithless people who have rejected the covenant. They had rejected God in spite of his great works of love on their behalf. Judgment resulted. The author of Hebrews draws his quotations from two parts of Deuteronomy 32:35–36:

> It is mine to avenge; I will repay.
>   In due time their foot will slip;
> their day of disaster is near
>   and their doom rushes upon them.
> The LORD will judge his people
>   and have compassion on his
>   servants
> when he sees their strength is gone
>   and no one is left, slave or free.

The first statement, "It is mine to avenge; I will repay," speaks of God's judgment on the wicked. The second, "The Lord will judge his people," sounds like a statement of vindication, but it too is given in the context of judgment. In Hebrews 10:31 the author speaks of the dreadfulness of falling into God's hands. The Song of Moses speaks further of the Lord's hand. No one can deliver out of his hand (Deut. 32:39); when his hand grasps the flashing sword for judgment, vengeance on his enemies is a sure thing (32:41).

Remember those earlier days (10:32). An important aspect of Greek rhetoric and ancient preaching was to use examples effectively. In 10:32–39 the author uses the hearers themselves as an example for endurance. That they had "stood [their] ground in a great contest in the face of suffering" suggests they had been persecuted severely.

A great contest in the face of suffering (10:32). The word translated "contest" (*athlēsis*) speaks of a difficult struggle, and commentators have pointed to the expulsion of Jews from Rome by the emperor Claudius in A.D. 49 as a possible backdrop for the experience mentioned here. At various points in the first century Jews were abused publicly as a group. Eviction from their homes was accompanied by looting of their possessions. It may be that the Christians, caught up in the conflict of Claudius's eviction, experienced various forms of persecution.

The author mentions in 10:32–34 that (1) they were "publicly exposed" to ridicule. The word translated "publicly exposed" (*theatrizō*) originally was associated with public performance, meaning to bring up on stage. As the language developed it took on the negative, figurative meaning evidenced here. Evidently these Christians had suffered both verbal and physical abuse. (2) Even when members were not being abused themselves, they suffered the emotional trauma of standing with those who were mistreated. (3) Their identification extended to those in prison, as members of the group sympathized with them. (4) Some of the believers had their property confiscated. The happy response to these persecutions, however, was joy. They celebrated the greater realities of God rather than focusing on the material problems of the moment. Such a perspective provides a solid foundation for Christian endurance.

He who is coming will come (10:37–38). The quotation in these two verses juxtaposes Isaiah 26:20–21 and Habakkuk 2:3–4, contrasting the righteous who live by faith in God and the wicked who reject him. Both Old Testament texts mention the "coming"—Isaiah says the Lord is coming, and Habakkuk proclaims the revelation of judgment is coming. In line with dominant twin motifs in Jewish thought, the righteous will be rewarded and the wicked punished. The author interprets these texts to refer to Christ's coming, an event for which the hearers must wait, demonstrating perseverance in the meantime. In the face of difficulties as they now stand with the community of faith, the author challenges them to choose faith and perseverance so they will receive the promises of God.

Overture (11:1–3)

Hebrews 11 constitutes one of the church's most loved portions of Scripture. The author sets before the reader a panoramic view of Old Testament history, highlighting significant events of that history involving faith. Much more than simply reminding his readers of interesting stories, he has a specific aim in the way he packages these narratives. For Hebrews 11 has the form of an ancient "example list," a rhetorical and preaching tool used to exhort listeners to take a specific course of action.[117] For example, the Jewish writer Philo has a similar list extolling the virtues of hope.[118] The aim is to give example after example of people who have taken the desired course of behavior, impressing the hearers with the positive outcome of their actions. Specifically in Hebrews 11, by providing those addressed with copious examples, the author challenges them to grasp that God's people must live by faith, and having grasped that truth, to live a life of persevering faith. Since the examples used in Hebrews 11 constitute great personages of the Old Testament, it is not surprising that these persons get press in the Jewish literature of our author's era.

By faith we understand that the universe was formed at God's command (11:3). One modern Jewish commentator calls creation "the fundamental affirmation of heirs of the biblical tradition."[119] In his *Antiquities* Josephus notes that Moses, in laying out the laws for humankind, does not start, like most lawgivers, with contracts and questions concerning rights, but rather with God and his creation of the world (1:21), thus laying a firm foundation for the giving of the law. This is the place to begin when discussing any subject worth discussing. *Joseph and Aseneth*, an ancient Jewish book of the Greco-Roman world, states that God is he "who brought the invisible (things) out into the light, who made the (things that) are and the (ones that) have an appearance from the non-appearing and non-being" (12:1–2). Faith grasps that the created order has resulted from the command of God and that what is seen, at times, relates directly to what is unseen.

Movement 1: First Examples of Faith (11:4–12)

By faith Abel (11:4). Abel, Adam and Eve's second son, was murdered by Cain, his brother, because his sacrifice was better than Cain's (Gen. 4:4–12). It may be that Abel's sacrifice was better because that sacrifice, "fat portions from some of

---

▶ What Is Faith?

Faith was a foundational component of Judaism in both Old Testament and postbiblical Judaism. Faith had to do with a posture of obedience (i.e., faithfulness to the covenant with God), and, closely related, trust in God. Greek philosophers often understood faith to be an inferior way of thinking, that is, "mere belief."[A-13] Yet, for the Jews of ancient Greco-Roman society, faith continued to be a key to relationship with God and was even called "the queen of virtues."[A-14] In Hebrews the author defines faith as "being sure of what we hope for and certain of what we do not see" (1:1). The term *hypostasis*, translated by the NIV as a participle ("being sure"), is in fact a noun with a range of meanings, including substance, firmness, confidence, guarantee, or proof. Given the examples of chapter 11, the definition can be translated as "faith is the firm confidence . . . ," since the exemplars listed have a resolute confidence in the unseen God.

the firstborn of his flock," reflected an attitude of Abel's heart. In line with this interpretation, Genesis 4:4 reports "the LORD looked in favor on Abel and his offering." Hebrews also proclaims "by faith" Abel "still speaks, even though he is dead." There is a strand of Jewish tradition that heralds Abel as one who continues to plead for vengeance on the descendants of Cain. *First Enoch*, a pre-Christian book, has Abel's spirit pleading with heaven to exterminate all of Cain's seed (22:5–7). In the *Testament of Abraham* 13:1–6 Abel sits as judge of all creation. At Hebrews 12:24 the author celebrates the fact that Jesus' blood speaks better than Abel's, proclaiming forgiveness rather than vengeance.

By faith Enoch (11:5). Genesis 5:24 reports Enoch's transportation from this life without experiencing death. That he was "commended as one who pleased God" is reflected in the Old Testament text as he "walked with God"—and he is the only one in that genealogy to receive such a description.

Without faith it is impossible to please God (11:6). This statement consists of a further reflection on the conflated quotation of Isaiah 26:20–21 and Habakkuk 2:3–4 in Hebrews 10:37–38. God is pleased with the one who exhibits faith and does not shrink back.

By faith Noah (11:7). Noah was the first to respond in faith to the Word of God (Gen. 6:1–9:17). The author of Hebrews places great emphasis on faith as acting in the face of what is not seen, and so he points out how Noah acted though the Flood was not yet seen. Consequently, by faith he became "[an] heir of . . . righteousness" and condemned those who

did not believe. Josephus comments that God loved Noah because of his righteousness, and *1 Enoch* 65–66 sees him as a prophet of cosmic judgment.[120]

By faith Abraham (11:8–12). Given the prominence of Abraham as a stellar example of faith in Jewish and early Christian traditions,[121] it is not surprising that the author of Hebrews gives extensive space to this patriarch as exemplar. Genesis 12:1–9 tells how Abraham obediently left his country and his father's house in order to pursue God's call to a new life. Hebrews again emphasizes that this act of obedience involved an unseen element since he went, "even though he did not know where he was going" (11:8). Furthermore, Abraham was a foreigner, who, as heir to God's promise, was looking for a city built by God himself (11:10). The fulfillment of God's promise not only involved a place but also a progeny. An old man and woman having a son demonstrates God's faithful response to faith (11:11–12).

Interlude: A Faith of Pilgrims (11:13–16)

Aliens and strangers on earth (11:13). The view that God's people are aliens and strangers in this world, who are looking for a heavenly city, has at its core an apocalyptic understanding of reality, yet it is based on an Old Testament motif. Passages like Genesis 23:4, 1 Chronicles 29:15, and Psalm 39:12 have the Old Testament faithful confessing that they are "aliens and strangers" on the earth. In both Jewish theology and early Christianity this concept developed to the idea that earthly passions are to be denied and the heavenly home is the believer's object of true affection.[122] Jewish apocalyptic emphasized the heavenly Jerusalem as the only true city, the only city that is eternal, since God is its builder.

Movement 2: More Examples of Faith (11:17–31)

By faith Abraham ... offered Isaac (11:17–18). Among Abraham's acts of faith, the offering of Isaac, also known as the *akedah* and recounted in Genesis 22:1–8, shines as the example of faith par excellence. This act is celebrated in Jewish tradition. For instance, *Jubilees*, a Jewish writing from the second century B.C., shares the story from the vantage point of the angel Mastema and concludes with the Lord saying to Abraham, "I have made known to all that you are faithful to me in everything which I say to you" (17:15–18:19). In a catalogue of Old Testament "famous men," Sirach 44:20 comments of Abraham: "When he was tested he proved faithful." Hebrews points out that Abraham's obedience

came in the face of an excruciating juxtaposition of the promises of God concerning his heir and the command of God to kill that heir. All the patriarch could do was trust God, and Hebrews states "Abraham reasoned that God could raise the dead." This is the only way that both the command and God's promises could be fulfilled.

By faith Isaac blessed Jacob and Esau (11:20). Hebrews deals briefly with the next three generations of the faithful. Why does the author not go into more detail? Remember that the "example list" form of exhortation is effective because of the quantity of evidence or the number of examples brought to bear. At this point the author is not interested in the details of each example but rather that each may be said to have exemplified faith in a specific, dynamic way. The blessing of Jacob and Esau by Isaac is found in Genesis 27:27–40. The ritual of blessing was considered a powerful act of bestowing or foretelling good and is at times contrasted with the concept of curse in the Old Testament. Jacob continued the ritual by blessing Joseph's sons, Ephraim and Manasseh (48:8–22). By faith Joseph, the great leader of Egypt, prophesied about the Exodus of the Israelites from the land of Egypt and instructed his descendants concerning the care of his bones (50:24–25). All of these acted in faith because they were speaking of as-yet unseen events.

By faith Moses (11:23–24). Moses held a special place in the hearts of first-century Jews, many of whom considered him to be the greatest person of history. He was understood to have achieved a unique intimacy with God, and some thought that the Messiah, when he came,

ROSETTA STONE

An Egyptian monument inscription dating to 196 B.C. written in hieroglyphic Egyptian, demotic Egyptian, and Greek.

would be a "new Moses."[123] Sirach 45:4–5, a book that dates from about 180 B.C., points out Moses' character as one who was faithful:

> For his faithfulness and meekness he
>   consecrated him,
>   choosing him out of all humankind.
> He allowed him to hear his voice,
>   and led him into the dark cloud,
> and gave him the commandments face
>   to face,
>   the law of life and knowledge,
> so that he might teach Jacob the
>   covenant,
>   and Israel his decrees.

Thus Moses' faithfulness to God was recognized in Judaism and lauded, as in Hebrews. The account of Moses in Hebrews 11 begins with the faith of his parents, who hid him from Pharaoh (Ex. 2:1–4).

Second, the faith of Moses himself is celebrated (Heb. 11:24–26) in that he rejected his adoptive mother, Pharaoh's daughter, in favor of solidarity with the people of God: "He regarded disgrace for the sake of Christ as of greater value than the treasures of Egypt" (11:26). The so-called "New Kingdom" of Egypt, which began in about 1552 B.C. and ended in 1069 B.C., saw the height of Egypt's political power and considerable wealth. It was a time of splendor and opulence. Yet, Moses rejected the Egyptian culture for the sake of suffering with God's people. So he left Egypt and "persevered because he saw him who is invisible" (11:27). Once again the author emphasizes perseverance based on the invisible God.

Finally, Moses kept the Passover, with its sprinkling of blood. Those in the congregation addressed by Hebrews who were of Jewish heritage undoubtedly grew up celebrating the Passover festival with its *haggadah*, or narrative, of the events surrounding the Exodus, focused on the Passover itself—the passing over of the houses of the Israelites who had placed blood on their doorposts.

By faith the people passed through the Red Sea (11:29). Recounted in Exodus 13:17–14:21, the crossing of the Red Sea does not seem at first glance to be illustrative of the faith of the people, who were often timid grumblers lacking trust in God (Heb. 3:7–19). Yet, the author considers acts of obedience carried out on God's command to be acts of faith, and the people did go forward when told to do so.

By faith the walls of Jericho fell (11:30). Joshua 5:13–6:27 records the conquering of Jericho. Obedience to the odd command to march around the city for seven days resulted in its walls falling down. The Old Testament city of Jericho normally is identified with the mound of Tell es-Sultan, northwest of the mouth of the Jordan River at the Dead Sea. The city was ancient even in Joshua's time and owed its location to a perennial spring. Walls were especially significant in ancient warfare, because they both gave a good defensive position (i.e., the top of the walls) and protection to those in the city. Thus the falling of Jericho's walls heralded God's act against the city and its inhabitants. The Israelites manifested faith by acting in obedience to a promise from the Lord, "See, I have delivered Jericho into your hands" (Josh. 6:2).

By faith the prostitute Rahab (11:31). Rahab plays a big part in the Jericho narrative. The prostitute had hidden the two spies during their reconnaissance of the land (Josh 2:1–24), and in return the spies had given an oath of protection to her and her family. When Jericho was destroyed, she and her family were saved. Prostitutes of the Old Testament era, either male or female, might be common prostitutes or sacred prostitutes of a pagan cult. Rahab seems to have been the former. The Joshua story demonstrates her belief in the power of Israel's God. She is noted as an ancestor of Jesus in Matthew 1:5, and James 2:25 points to the activeness of her faith as commendable and an illustration of true faith.

Crescendo and Conclusion (11:32–40)

What more shall I say? (11:32). This stylized question is found widely in classical oratorical literature of the period, as well as being used extensively by Philo of Alexandria.[124] It is a way of the author turning a corner from his methodical example list offered thus far and moving toward a conclusion.

I do not have time to tell about ... (11:32). The author of Hebrews now gives a concise summary of Old Testament and, perhaps, intertestament acts of faith. Six heroes from the era of the judges and united monarchy begin the summary, with the general designation "the prophets" tacked on. The six names are not in chronological order, but each brings to mind a history of valor lived out in faith under the rule of the unseen God. Gideon and his three hundred routed the Midianites with torches and jars (Judg. 7:7–25). A military leader under the judge Deborah, Barak defeated Sisera and the Canaanites (4:8–16). Samson championed the Israelites' cause during the Philistine crisis (13:1–16:31), and Jephthah, who made a horrific vow of

sacrifice, defeated the Amorites and Ammonites (10:6–12:7). Samuel, the bridge figure between the time of the judges and the united monarchy, discerned God's voice, and David, the only king mentioned here, lived a life of devotion to God and did great acts of faith. "The prophets" covers numerous figures who lived faithfully for God, mostly in the face of hostile cultures.

Shut the mouths of lions ... (11:33–35). The great heroes of faith at times saw positive outcomes of their faith. An obvious reference to Daniel, the author states that some of them "shut the mouths of lions." Daniel 6:23 says that "no wound was found on him, because he had trusted in his God." Shadrach, Meshach, and Abednego probably are in view as those who "quenched the fury of the flames" (cf. 3:16–30). Other prophets such as Elijah, Elisha, and Jeremiah "escaped the edge of the sword" by their faith. In the Old Testament women such as the widow of Zarephath and the woman of Shunem had sons who were resuscitated from death by Elijah and Elisha respectively (1 Kings 17:17–24; 2 Kings 4:17–37).

Others were tortured ... (11:35b–38). The outcomes of faith were not always positive by this world's values. Some in faith "were tortured and refused to be released, so that they might gain a better resurrection." During the first century, Jews who suffered under Roman oppression held heroes from the Maccabean era in high esteem because of their opposition to Greek rule in the first half of the second century B.C. Perhaps the author of Hebrews has some of these heroes in mind at this point. Second Maccabees 6 tells of a horrible time during which the

Greeks attempted to force pagan religion on the Jewish people, defiling the temple and forcing the Jews to disobey divine law. Eleazar, a ninety-year-old scribe, in the face of a death penalty, refused to eat pork, even as friends encouraged him to "fake it" by using another type of meat. At his death he stated, "It is clear to the Lord in his holy knowledge that, though I might have been saved from death, I am enduring terrible sufferings in my body under this beating, but in my soul I am glad to suffer these things because I fear him" (2 Macc. 6:30).

In 2 Maccabees 7, a mother and her seven sons die nobly under horrible torture. The first son, before the eyes of his family, has his tongue cut out, is scalped, and has his hands and feet cut off. Finally, he is fried in a pan until he dies. The second son dies in the same way, but with his last breath says, "You accursed wretch, you dismiss us from this present life, but the King of the universe will raise us up to an everlasting renewal of life, because we have died for his laws" (2 Macc. 7:9).

According to tradition, the prophet Jeremiah was "stoned" and Isaiah was "sawed in two."[125] Clement of Rome, in *1 Clement* 17:1, points to Elijah, Elisha, and Ezekiel as those who wore "sheepskins and goatskins," who were "destitute, persecuted and mistreated," wandering "in deserts and mountains, and in caves and holes in the ground." These words are also descriptive of the Jews of the Maccabean revolt who were persecuted under Antiochus IV Epiphanes.

The author of Hebrews points out that the world was not worthy of these great people of faith, who lived out their commitment to the unseen God in the face of hostility. God commended them for their faith, meaning he bore witness to their faith. The conclusion the author of Hebrews wishes the reader to draw is that faith is the only way to live for God.

Enduring Under Trial (12:1–17)

The author of Hebrews has already shown the connection between faith and endurance under adverse circumstances in 10:32–39 and given numerous examples of faithful endurance in chapter 11. Now the author adds a metaphor (the race imagery of 12:1–2, 12–13), an analogy (parental discipline in 12:3–11), and a negative example (Esau in 12:14–17), all of which extend his treatment of endurance as a Christian virtue.

Cloud of witnesses (12:1). The "cloud of witnesses" refers to the exemplars of Hebrews 11. Writers of classical literature used cloud imagery to describe a large throng of people. That they are a "cloud of witnesses" has prompted some to envision the faithful of Hebrews 11 as sitting in the stands of eternity, observing contemporary Christians in their struggle. The word we translate "witness" can connote "spectator" (e.g., 1 Tim. 6:12), and *perikeimenon*, translated as "surrounded," perhaps brings to mind the ancient amphitheater. Yet, it is doubtful

R E F L E C T I O N S

IN MODERN, WESTERN CHRISTIANITY FAITH OFTEN is tied to positive outcomes. In the so-called "health and wealth" gospel, negative outcomes only happen to those who do not have sufficient faith. Hebrews 11 dispels this theological myth. Yes, God does answer immediately in certain situations, but the faithful may also face severe persecution for which there seems no immediate answer. Is your concept of faith big enough to encompass both the triumphs and tragedies of life?

that the author sees the ancient faithful as passive spectators. Rather, as a "cloud of witnesses" they bear witness to God's faithfulness to the faithful. As such they offer great encouragement to Christians struggling to endure in faith.

Throw off everything that hinders ... and let us run (12:1). The use of athletic imagery to speak to the need for endurance in suffering or virtue is widespread in both Greco-Roman and Jewish literature.[126] For instance, extolling the virtues of piety and faith for the virtuous person, Philo, the Alexandrian Jew of the first century, states:

> If, however, as he goes on his way, he neither becomes weary, so that he gives in and collapses, nor grows remiss, so that he turns aside, now in this direction, now in that, and goes astray missing the central road that never diverges; but, taking the good runners as his example, finishes the race of life without stumbling, when he has reached the end he shall obtain crowns and prizes as a fitting guerdon [reward].[127]

In another place Philo proclaims that physical contests, such as foot races, are laughable, because most small or large beasts would be able to defeat a human. He suggests that the only contest that is worth the effort is

> the contest for the winning of the virtues which are divine and really

A VICTORIOUS RUNNER

The athlete holds the crown of victory.

▶ The Discipline of a Father in the Ancient World

The Jews, Greeks, and Romans of the ancient world embraced the concept of paternal authority, yet this authority often was wielded in a context of love and nurture. From literary sources we know that fathers often were involved in the day-to-day aspects of raising their children. For example, Aeschylus writes of the challenge one faces in determining what a young child wants, Horace acknowledges the balkiness of two-year-olds, and Euripides speaks of a child's fear of being abandoned.[A-15] Early childhood was seen as a significant stage of development in which the child was moldable. Children were seen as needing to play, eat well, be clothed adequately, loved, protected, and disciplined.

The father had the ultimate responsibility of training his son. Although in wealthier families a tutor might be used in the care and training of a boy after age six or seven, the continued role of the father was paramount (cf. 1 Cor. 4:15). The father trained his son so as to prepare him for adult life, and this training often involved correction and punishment. In Jewish literature this picture of the father who disciplines for the good of the child can be seen in the Wisdom tradition,[A-16] and the image is extended to the Lord as the one who corrects his children out of love.[A-17] Thus Hebrews is heir to this tradition.

Olympian. For this contest those who are very weaklings in their bodies but stalwarts in their souls all enter, and proceed to strip and rub dust over them and do everything that skill and strength enables them to do, omitting nothing that can help them to victory.[128]

So too the author of Hebrews challenges his readers to "strip" off everything that hinders them in the race of endurance. An ancient writer could use the term *onkos*, translated in 12:1 as [something] "that hinders," to refer to a mass, weight, or bodily fat. In the context of running, it could refer to burdensome clothing or excess bodily weight. There-fore, believers are to run the Christian race with endurance, laying aside those things that bind or weigh us down.

Scorning its shame (12:2). The Greek word *kataphroneō*, rendered as "scorning" by the NIV, means to treat someone or something as though he or it had little value. Jesus uses the word when he speaks to the impossibility of serving two masters (Matt. 6:24): One master will be loved and the other "scorned." When the author of Hebrews says that Jesus "endured the cross, scorning its shame," he uses power-ful imagery to which hearers of the first century would have been attuned. Cruci-fixion was the lowest form of capital pun-ishment in the ancient world, reserved for slaves and criminals and consisting of a perverse mix of humiliation and torture. As such, it was a most intense form of scorning. In crucifixion the Roman and Jewish officials treated Jesus as valueless. What Jesus did was to "scorn this shame" by looking beyond it to the joy at the Father's right hand. He, therefore, serves as the ultimate example for those who suffer under persecution.

You have forgotten that word of encour-agement that addresses you as sons (12:5). In 12:5–6 the author quotes Proverbs 3:11–12, which puts "discipline" in a positive framework. The Lord's disci-pline and rebuke are indications of his love and commitment to believers as "sons." Hebrews 12:7 makes clear that the author understands the hardship the hearers are facing to be synonymous with the Lord's discipline. They are to endure it and per-ceive it as a mark of their legitimacy as God's children (12:8).

Strengthen your feeble arms and weak knees (12:12). Hebrews picks up once

REFLECTIONS

IT DOES NOT TAKE LONG EXPERI-ence in the Christian faith to learn that maintaining a resolute commitment to Christ is not easy and demands endurance. We can find help, however, from several directions. The "cloud of wit-nesses" reminds us that God's people of the past have walked similar paths as the ones we are walking presently and have done so keeping faith. The exhortation of Scripture to put off those things that hin-der us reminds us that the weights we embrace in life—whether unwholesome activities or attitudes of questionable value—can impede our progress in the faith. Finally, we must look to Jesus as the ultimate example of endurance. His atti-tude of scorning shame gives us a pow-erful reference point from which to evaluate the difficulties of life, especially those that come because we are commit-ted to God's path.

again on the athletic imagery used earlier in the chapter, this time drawing from Isaiah 35:3 and Proverbs 4:26. The phrase "feeble arms and weak knees" serves as a metaphor for emotional and spiritual fatigue, which the persecuted first hearers of Hebrews must have been feeling.

According to Isaiah 35:3–8, the imagery of strengthening weak knees and hands is connected to the idea of hope in the Lord, who will come with retribution on Israel's enemies and salvation for his people. The message, therefore, is one of encouragement and consideration of God's holy way—to continue to walk in the Lord's path and to endure until he brings deliverance.

Drawing a connection in Hebrews 12:13 to the concept of the right path, the author quotes Proverbs 4:26: "Make level paths for your feet." The straight and level path serves as a common image for God's way of right living. Paths that are full of holes and bumps are dangerous, especially for a person who already is lame. The verb *ektrepō* is often translated "turn aside, go astray," but "disabled" is appropriate. Writers of the ancient world sometimes used the word to refer to dislocation.[129] All paths other than the Lord's path are dangerous; only his path leads to health.

Bitter root (12:15). Continuing with a theme of right living, the author alludes to the "bitter root" of Deuteronomy 29:18: "Make sure there is no man or woman, clan or tribe among you today whose heart turns away from the LORD our God to go and worship the gods of those nations; make sure there is no root among you that produces such bitter poison." The Old Testament context holds great significance for understanding the

author's concerns at this point in Hebrews. In Deuteronomy, Moses is renewing the covenant prior to the crossing into the Promised Land. He challenges the Israelites not to turn away from the covenant. In the larger context of Hebrews the concern is that the hearers not turn away from the superior covenant offered by Christ.

Godless like Esau (12:16). Although the biblical text does not say specifically that Esau was "sexually immoral," some strands of Jewish interpretation describe him as sexually questionable because of his marriage to the Hittites Judith and Basemath (Gen. 26:34).[130] The word translated "godless" describes something that is unholy or base. Esau was godless because of his misplaced values, shown by his emphasis on food; in this Old Testament incident Esau betrays a heart that does not value the greater values of God.

Inheritance rights as the oldest son (12:16). The receiving of an inheritance from one's father was a socio-legal practice throughout the ancient world. Deuteronomy 21:16–17 says that a first-born son receives a double portion of the father's inheritance, and this is what Esau treated so lightly (Gen. 25:29–34).

Inherit this blessing (12:17). Adding insult to injury, Jacob not only garnered Esau's birthright, but also took his blessing by deceiving their father (27:30–40). At their heart, Old Testament blessings, such as the one found in this narrative, are words of power, meant to impact the future of the child blessed. Isaac's blessing of Jacob was so comprehensive that he could not similarly bless Esau (27:36–38). The author of Hebrews wishes to point out by analogy that once an inheritance and blessing have been rejected, only tears and rejection result. Believers, rather, should value their inheritance.

A Contrast of Two Covenants (12:18–29)

A rich tradition of biblical imagery lies behind the contrast of Mount Sinai and Mount Zion at 12:18–24. Mountains often are significant sacred sites where people meet God.[131] The author of Hebrews has already dealt with the ratification of the covenant at Mount Sinai, and that experience of the Israelites, with Moses going up into the cloud to meet with God, is symbolic of the old covenant. As biblical history developed, with the movement of God's people into the Promised Land, Mount Zion, on which the temple stood in Jerusalem, displaced Mount Sinai as God's residence on earth.[132] In keeping with his orientation to apocalyptic Judaism, however, the author of Hebrews contrasts the earthly Sinai with the heavenly Mount Zion.

A mountain that can be touched (12:18). Though the author of Hebrews never mentions Mount Sinai by name, he clearly has this significant Old Testament mountain in view and draws his descriptive language in this passage from the desert wanderers' encounter with God as told in Exodus and Deuteronomy.[133] The event is Israel's drawing near to God in solemn assembly to covenant with him (Deut. 4:10–14). Strikingly visual and aural, the language in Hebrews 12:18–21 (fire, darkness, gloom, storm, trumpet blast, and the voice) is at the same time impersonal and terrible.

The auditory manifestations—the "trumpet blast" and the "voice speaking words"—were especially terrifying. The sound of the trumpet filled the air around Mount Sinai on the morning of the third day at the mountain, and it grew louder and louder, causing the Israelites to tremble with fear (Ex. 19:16, 19; 20:18). The "voice speaking words" came from the fire (Deut. 4:12), and the people, not seeing God but hearing the

disembodied voice, begged that God would be quiet (Ex. 20:18–19; Deut. 5:23–27). The message of Hebrews 12:18–21, therefore, is that one must keep one's distance and not come near to God. After all, this is a mountain that "can be touched," but the consequences for doing so are disastrous: "Whoever touches the mountain shall surely be put to death" (Ex. 19:12).

But you have come to Mount Zion (12:22). By contrast, the participants in the new covenant have come to Mount Zion, the dwelling place of God, a place of relationships. Mount Zion and the city of Jerusalem are so closely related in biblical literature that the two at times are practically synonymous, representing the dwelling place of God. Notice the poetic parallelism in passages like Joel 2:32 and Micah 4:2. Amos 1:2 states, "The LORD roars from Zion and thunders from Jerusalem." In keeping with the author's apocalyptic framework, the city to which new covenanters have come is the heavenly Jerusalem, the "heavenly . . . city" mentioned in Hebrews 11:16 and the "city that is to come" of 13:14.

Thousands of angels in joyful assembly (12:22). Believers also have come to a host of angels. The term *panēgyris*, translated in 12:22 as "in joyful assembly" and only found here in the New Testament, was used in secular literature of parties or the atmosphere of celebration at the annual athletic competitions. In the LXX, the term connotes a gathering, often at festival time, to celebrate with joy and delight.[134]

The sprinkled blood that speaks a better word than the blood of Abel (12:24). Having gone to great lengths to demon-strate that the blood of Christ cleanses completely and forever from sin (8:7–13; 9:11–14; 10:15–18), the author makes a striking statement that Jesus' blood "speaks." What does he mean that it speaks better than Abel's blood? After Cain had killed Abel, Abel's blood "cried out" to God from the ground for judgment (Gen. 4:10), a figurative way of saying that the murder must be met with justice. Furthermore, *1 Enoch* 22:5–7 says Abel continued to plead for vengeance on the descendants of Cain, wishing all of his brother's seed to be exterminated. Based on the Old Testament text's confession of Abel's blood as speaking, the author of Hebrews proclaims that Jesus' blood speaks a "better word." Whereas Abel's blood cries out for justice, Christ's blood cries out that justice has been met by his sacrifice for sins. His blood, in other words, says, "forgiven."

Once more I will shake not only the earth but also the heavens (12:26). The "time" in view here is again the manifestation of God's awesomeness at Mount Sinai.[135] Now the author turns attention to a time in the future, quoting Haggai 2:6 and weaving elements of interpretation into his quotation. The Old Testament text reads, "In a little while I will shake the heavens and the earth." This passage includes both the shaking of earth, a manifestation that occurred in relation to Mount Sinai, and the shaking of heaven. Thus, to emphasize the point, the author of Hebrews reverses the words "heaven" and "earth" and inserts the connectives "not only . . . but also": "Once more I will shake not only the earth but also the heavens." This cosmic shaking speaks of the eschatological judgment brought on the earth at the end of the age, when the material universe will pass from the scene.[136]

General Guidelines for Christian Living (13:1–6)

Keep on loving each other as brothers (13:1). The word *philadelphia*, translated by the NIV as "loving . . . as brothers" was a common ethical term in early Christianity.[137] As the word is used in its various contexts it speaks to the meeting of one another's needs and is part of a larger theological complex that understands love as the foundational Christian posture.[138]

Remember those in prison (13:3). In ancient Rome there were both public prisons and private homes used as jails. While the latter were used primarily for holding slaves, the former had various uses, including the detainment of those awaiting trial and those awaiting execution.[139] An infamous part of the prison system in Rome was the *Tullianum*, which consisted of an upper and a lower vault. The lower vault could be reached only through a hole in the ceiling. Sallust describes the *Tullianum* as follows:

There is in the prison a chamber named the Tullianum, about twelve feet below the surface of the earth. It is surrounded by walls, and covered by a vaulted roof of stone; but its appearance is repulsive and fearful, because of the neglect, the darkness, and the stench.[140]

This chamber is the traditional site of the imprisonments of Paul and Peter. If Hebrews was originally addressed to Christians in Rome, as we have suggested, the readers would have been familiar with the harshness of the prisons. Prisoners were not treated well in the first century and often had to depend on family and friends for basic needs.[141] Consolation, gifts such as food, and

▶ Hospitality in the Ancient World

One of the foremost rules of brotherly love in the Christian churches was to show hospitality, especially perhaps to traveling preachers of the gospel.[A-18] Hospitality constitutes the act of making strangers welcome in one's home, caring for their needs as one would a friend. In the ancient world the cost of staying at an inn was prohibitive for most, and such establishments usually had poor reputations as hangouts for prostitutes and thieves. Thus hospitality became highly valued in Greco-Roman as well as Jewish society, and these form the backdrop of the Christian ethic.

Junia Theodora, for instance, a Roman citizen living in Corinth in mid-first-century A.D., was honored by the Lycian confederation and by the people of Telmessos because of her hospitality. The decree states that she "tirelessly showed zeal and generosity toward the Lycian nation and was kind to all travelers, private individuals as well as ambassadors, sent by the nation or the various cities."[A-19] The value placed on hospitality in Jewish society can be seen in passages such as *Test. Job* 10, which probably was written in the first century B.C. or A.D.:

And I established in my house thirty tables spread at all hours, for strangers only. I also used to maintain twelve other tables set for the widows. When any stranger approached to ask alms, he was required to be fed at my table before he would receive his need. Neither did I allow anyone to go out of my door with an empty pocket.

Many Jews regarded Abraham as the paradigm par excellence for hospitality. Writers such as Philo and Josephus lauded his hospitality shown to the angelic visitors (Gen. 18:2–15), to which the writer of Hebrews seems to allude in 13:2.

prayers all would have been greatly valued.[142] Therefore, the author of Hebrews challenges this congregation to "remember those in prison as if you were their fellow prisoners."

Marriage should be honored by all (13:4). The Jewish and Christian ethic of fidelity in marriage was attacked from two sides in the ancient world. On the one hand, some social commentators of the day felt chastity in marriage was unreasonable. Men, for instance, were expected to take mistresses as confidants and sexual partners. On the other hand, there were those holding to asceticism. To "honor" marriage means to "hold it as especially valuable." Correspondingly, the marriage bed is to be kept pure from sexual immorality and adultery. The latter concept refers to those who break their marriage vows by having sexual relations with someone other than their spouse. The former word, *pornoi*, addresses any sexual activity outside the context of marriage.

Keep your lives free from the love of money (13:5). The New Testament links sexual impurity and the love of money in several places, perhaps because the topics are addressed side by side as the seventh

right ▶
ROMAN GOLD
COINS

and eighth of the Ten Commandments.[143] To abstain from the love of money was extolled as a virtue in the broader Greco-Roman culture. Money was thought to corrupt government officials, for example, so one who was not a lover of money was seen as having the ability to manage objectively. The author of Hebrews challenges his hearers to "be content." Part of the background here may be the seizing of the believers' properties, which the author mentions at Hebrews 10:32–34.

Guidelines on Church Leadership and Doctrine (13:7–19)

Remember the leaders (13:7). Among the books of the New Testament, Hebrews alone refers to the church's officials as "leaders" (*hoi hegoumenoi*), although Acts 15:22 uses the same Greek word as an adjective to describe the "men" sent as a delegation to Antioch. The term was used in the broader culture of state officials and in the LXX for religious, political, and military leaders. The word also is used in the *Shepherd of Hermas* and *1 Clement*, early Christian documents associated with the city of Rome.

Ceremonial foods . . . an altar (13:9–10). Special cultic meals were practiced in some branches of first-century Judaism,

R E F L E C T I O N S

NOTICE THAT THE ETHIC REFLECTED IN HEBREWS 13:1–6 begins with a focus on the needs of others. What are ways in which you are expressing "brotherly love?" The need for hospitality, perhaps, takes different forms in modern contexts, but the foundational need to minister to God's people with our resources remains the principle of concern. Furthermore, there are many places in the world today in which brothers and sisters in Christ are suffering for the faith, many being put in prison. How might we apply 13:3 to their situation?

especially the fellowship meal, which was understood as communicating the grace of God. Giving God blessing, thanksgiving for his grace, and prayers of petition were all involved in such a meal. Jewish meals in general were understood to give the participants spiritual strength through the joy experienced at the table (Ps. 104:14–15). Meals gave faithful Jews the opportunity to reflect on God's goodness and provision and were meant to remind the faithful that the ultimate expression of thanks to God for redemption must be made in the thank offering and the fellowship meal at the Jerusalem altar. It may be, therefore, that some addressed by Hebrews were tempted to abandon the Christian meals, in which the grace of God through Christ was celebrated, in favor of Jewish meals that celebrated the altar in Jerusalem.[144]

The bodies are burned outside the camp . . . Jesus also suffered outside the city gate (13:11–12). The author has dealt extensively with the Day of Atonement sacrifices under the old covenant and Christ's superior atoning offering on the cross (9:11–14, 24–28; 10:1–4). The reference to "bodies . . . burned outside the camp" alludes to Leviticus 16:27, part of the instructions for the Day of Atonement offerings: "The bull and the goat for the sin offerings, whose blood was brought into the Most Holy Place to make atonement, must be taken outside the camp; their hides, flesh and offal are to be burned up." Drawing a parallel between the old covenant sacrifices and Jesus' experience, the writer notes that Jesus "suffered outside the city gate." The image is one of rejection. Crucifixion was a means of killing through torture and humiliation (Heb. 6:6; 12:2). Therefore, believers are to reject the comfort of

associating with the world, particularly the religion of Judaism, and embrace the disgrace of Christ.

Sacrifice of praise (13:15). This phrase occurs in the LXX at Leviticus 7:12, referring to the highest form of peace offering under the old covenant.[145] The thank offering, as the name implies, was given to express gratitude to God; it was voluntary and could only be made after the worshiper had been made ritually clean. As Christians we give this offering "through Jesus" and "continually" since he has cleansed us once for all time. The phrase "fruit of lips" also is associated with thanksgiving, especially in Psalms (e.g., Ps. 50:14, 23; 107:22).

Closing (13:20–25)

Hebrews generally has the form of a first-century sermon rather than a letter (see the Introduction); yet an epistolary ending was attached to this sermon, perhaps so it could be sent to the congregation by courier. Early Christian letters follow the general form of letters in the broader Greco-Roman culture, often containing a postscript meant to maintain the relationship between the sender and the recipient.[146] The Christian expression of the form includes some or all of the following elements: requests, a benediction, doxology, comments on the work's contents, personal news, greetings, and a farewell wish.[147] Hebrews includes all of these but the first.

May the God of peace (13:20). Benedictions were important both to letters and to other forms of address such as sermons, and in Jewish contexts were considered an act of worship.[148] An author could form his benediction to express specific needs of his hearers, as the author of Hebrews does in 13:20–21. The themes of the blood, the eternal covenant, and doing God's will are all important for Hebrews. The benediction, therefore, expresses the author's deep prayers for his hearers, especially that they may have a dynamic relationship with the great Shepherd, Jesus.

Shepherd of the sheep (13:20). The image of the shepherd has its roots in the pastoral setting of the Old Testament and is expressed poignantly with passages such as Psalm 23. The image developed in broader Jewish contexts of the Greco-Roman world, for instance, expressing hopes concerning the coming Messiah: "And the blessing of the Lord will be with him in strength, and he will not weaken; His hope (will be) in the Lord. Then who will succeed against him, mighty in his actions and strong in the fear of God? Faithfully and righteously shepherding the Lord's flock, he will not let any of them stumble in their pasture" (*Ps. Sol.* 17.40). Philo, moreover, applied the image to the divine Logos (*Agric.* 51). In the New Testament the Gospel of John picks up the image in 10:11–18, and 1 Peter 2:25 calls Jesus the "Shepherd and Overseer of your souls."

ANNOTATED BIBLIOGRAPHY

Attridge, Harold. *To the Hebrews.* Hermeneia. Philadelphia: Fortress, 1989.

A technical but clearly written commentary, which offers a wealth of information and a balanced treatment of the text at most points. After Lane, this is the best English-language commentary available.

Bruce, F. F. *The Epistle to the Hebrews*, revised ed. NICNT. Grand Rapids: Eerdmans, 1990.

Prior to the publication of the technical commentaries by Lane and Attridge, this volume, originally published in 1963, was the best English-language work available, with that by Hughes running a close second. As usual, Bruce offers outstanding, evangelical scholarship in the task of elucidating the New Testament.

Ellingworth, Paul. *Commentary on Hebrews.* NIGTC. Grand Rapids: Eerdmans, 1993.

An outstanding source of information, which, with the technical commentaries of Lane and Attridge, should be consulted. However, Ellingworth's treatment often misses important contextual concerns and shows too little sensitivity to the overall structure of Hebrews.

Guthrie, George H. *Hebrews.* NIVAC. Grand Rapids: Zondervan, 1998.

My own attempt at commenting on Hebrews. The approach follows the pattern for the series, addressing original meaning, bridging the contexts of the ancient and modern world, and application. Evangelical in orientation, the book seeks to be accessible by pastors and laypeople while addressing more technical issues such as structure and word meanings.

Hagner, Donald A. *Hebrews.* NIBC. Peabody, Mass.: Hendrickson, 1990.

This is a solid, evangelical, medium-level commentary that offers consistently helpful insights to the book.

Hughes, Philip E. *A Commentary on the Epistle to the Hebrews.* Grand Rapids: Eerdmans, 1977.

Not as detailed as Bruce in some respects but more inclined to deal with wide-ranging theological issues in the course of commentary. Prior to Lane and Attridge, with the exception of Bruce, Hughes offers the most helpful English-language commentary on the text of Hebrews.

Lane, William L. *Hebrews: Call to Commitment.* Peabody, Mass.: Hendrickson, 1985.

A popular treatment from one of the foremost scholars on Hebrews.

_____. *Hebrews 1–8* and *Hebrews 9–13.* WBC. Dallas: Word, 1991.

These two volumes are the best detailed exegetical commentary available today. Lane offers the most extensive and helpful introduction on the book available.

Main Text Notes

1. E.g., Rom. 1:1; 1 Cor. 15:8; Gal. 1:11–16.
2. Eusebius, *Eccl. Hist.* 6.25.14
3. For more on the structure of the book see George H. Guthrie, *Hebrews* (NIVAC; 1998), 27–31.
4. Aristotle, *The "Art" of Rhetoric*, trans. John Henry Freese (LCL; Cambridge, Mass.: Harvard Univ. Press, 1982), 427.
5. Philo, *On the Account of the World's Creation Given by Moses*, trans. F. H. Colson and G. H. Whitaker (LCL; Cambridge, Mass.: Harvard Univ. Press, 1981), 7.
6. Cf. Luke 1:55; Acts 3:13; 7:38–39; Harold W. Attridge, *The Epistle to the Hebrews* (Hermeneia; Philadelphia: Fortress, 1989), 38.
7. See, e.g., Plato, *Timaeus* 71e–72b.
8. C. H. Peisker, "Prophet," *NIDNTT*, 3:84–85.
9. E.g., Isa. 2:2–21; Joel 1–3; Amos 8:9–11; 9:9–12.
10. E.g., 2 Tim. 3:1; James 5:3; 2 Peter 3:3.
11. E.g., 4QFlor. 1:12.
12. Michael Grant and Rachel Kitzinger, eds., *Civilization of the Ancient Mediterranean: Greece and Rome* (New York: Charles Scribner's Sons, 1988), 3:1349.
13. B. F. Westcott, *The Epistle to the Hebrews: The Greek Text with Notes and Essays* (London: MacMillan, 1892), 168.
14. E.g., Ex. 16:7; 33:18; Isa. 40:5.
15. Donald Hagner, *Hebrews* (NIBC; Peabody, Mass.: Hendrickson, 1990), 23.
16. Philo, *Creation* 146.
17. E.g., Luke 9:32; John 1:14; 2:11; 17:5; Rom. 8:17; Phil. 3:21.
18. James Hope Moulton and George Milligan, *The Vocabulary of the Greek New Testament Illustrated from the Papyri and Other Non-Literary Sources* (London: Hodder and Stoughton, 1949), 683; Henry George Liddell and Robert Scott, *A Greek-English Lexicon*, revised by Henry Stuart Jones (Oxford: Clarendon, 1996, 1977).
19. Westcott, *Hebrews*, 12.
20. William Lane, *Hebrews 1–8* (WBC; Dallas: Word, 1991), 13.
21. E.g., John 1:14; Phil. 2:6; Col. 1:15.
22. Ps. 33:6; Isa. 40:26; 48:13.
23. Pindar, *Hymn 2, to Apollo*, line 29.
24. Theodor Herzl Gaster, *Myth, Legend, and Custom in the Old Testament: A Comparative Study with Chapters from Sir James Frazier's Folklore in the Old Testament* (New York: Harper & Row, 1969), 773–80.
25. Sigmund Mowinckel, "General Oriental and Specific Israelite Elements in the Israelite Conception of the Sacral Kingdom," in *The Sacral Kingship*, ed. G. Widengren (Leiden: Brill, 1959), 287.
26. E.g., Matt. 22:44; Acts 2:33; 5:31; Rom. 8:34; 1 Cor. 15:25.
27. P. Oxy. 1.58, MM, 451.
28. Richard Longenecker, *The Christology of Early Jewish Christianity* (Grand Rapids: Baker, 1981), 41–46.
29. Duane A. Garrett, *Angels and the New Spirituality* (Nashville, Tenn.: Broadman and Holman, 1995), 12–17.
30. Longenecker, *Christology*, 95. See Robert H. Eisenman and Michael Wise, *The Dead Sea Scrolls Uncovered* (Rockport, Mass.: Element, 1992), 70.
31. E.g., Acts 4:23–31; 13:33–34.
32. E.g., Ex. 13:2; 22:29; Lev. 27:26; Num. 3:13.
33. Ceslas Spicq, *Theological Lexicon of the New Testament*, trans. James D. Ernest, 3 vols. (Peabody, Mass.: Hendrickson, 1994), 3:210; e.g., 2 Sam. 13:36–37; 1 Chron. 3:1.
34. Rom. 8:29; Col. 1:15, 18; Heb. 12:23; Rev. 1:5.
35. A. A. Anderson, *Psalms (73–150)* (NCBC; Grand Rapids: Eerdmans, 1972), 719; Hans-Joachim Kraus, *Psalms 60–150: A Continental Commentary*, trans. Hilton C. Oswald (Minneapolis, Minn.: Fortress, 1993), 299–300; Franz Delitzsch, *Biblical Commentary on the Psalms*, trans. Francis Bolton (Grand Rapids, Mich.: Eerdmans, 1959), 3:129–30.
36. J. A. Thompson, *Handbook of Life in Bible Times* (Downers Grove, Ill.: InterVarsity, 1986), 274.
37. Attridge, *Hebrews*, 60.
38. J. Douglas et al., eds., *New Bible Dictionary*, 2d ed. (Downers Grove, Ill.: InterVarsity, 1982), 394; 1 Kings 5:17; 6:37; 7:10.
39. Westcott, *Hebrews*, 36–37; Aristotle, *De partibus animalium* 3.3; R. C. H. Lenski, *The Interpretation of the Epistle to the Hebrews and the Epistle of James* (Columbus, Ohio: Wartburg, 1946), 64.
40. So Lane, *Hebrews 1–8*, 35, 37, who follows P. Teodrico, "Metafore nautiche in *Ebr.* 2, 1 e 6, 19," *RB* 6 (1958): 33–49. Herodotus (e.g., 2.150; 6.20) and Strabo (9.2.31) speak of the flow of a body of water past some point.
41. Josephus, *Ant.* 15.5.5 §136.
42. Deissmann, *Bible Studies*, 107–9.
43. Philo, *Moses* 2.14.
44. Num. 35:16–21; Lev. 20:10; Deut. 22:24; Lev. 20:11–14; Ex. 22:19; Lev. 18:22; 20:13.

45. Job 34:11; Ps. 62:12; Prov. 24:12; Ezek. 7:3, 27; Job 11:20; Prov. 1:24–31; Jer. 11:11.
46. E.g., Acts 2:22; Rom. 15:19; 2 Cor. 12:12.
47. Stephens, *The New Testament World in Pictures*, 24.
48. Attridge, *Hebrews*, 87–88; Lane, *Hebrews 1– 8*, 56–57.
49. Ex. 29:9, 29, 33, 35; Lev. 8:33; 16:32; Num. 3:3.
50. Matt. 27:35; John 19:23, 31–36.
51. Epictetus, *Diss.* 1.27.9–10
52. Spicq, *TLNT*, 2:478–781.
53. Grant and Kitzinger, *Civilization of the Ancient Mediterranean*, 1:299–308; 3:1373– 76.
54. E.g., Num. 32:7–11; Deut. 1:19–35; Neh. 9:15–17; Ps. 106:24–26; *4 Ezra* 7:106.
55. 1 Cor. 10:6–12.
56. Lane, *Hebrews 1–8*, 84–85.
57. Cf. Ex. 4:14; 7:3; 8:15; Ezek. 11:19.
58. Cf. also Rom. 8:17; 11:22; 2 Cor. 13:5b.
59. Cf. Matt. 7:15–23; James 2:14–26.
60. Ibid., 84.
61. Num. 14:1–38; Deut. 9; Ps. 78:22, 32; 106.
62. E.g., Deut. 3:20; 12:9; Josh. 1:13, 15; Isa. 63:14.
63. Ronald Williamson, *Philo and the Epistle to the Hebrews* (ALGHJ; 1970), 547–48.
64. E.g., Ex. 16:23, 30; 31:15; 34:21; 35:2.
65. Lev. 16:29–31; 23:26–28, 32.
66. Garland Young, "A Soldier's Armor," *BI* 21 (Fall 1994): 38.
67. Leland Ryken et al., *DBI* (1998), 835.
68. Martin Hengel, *The Son of God* (Philadelphia: Fortress), 30. Hengel's work devastated earlier suggestions that Christianity borrowed its concept of Jesus as God's dying and rising son from broader Greek mythology.
69. E.g., Matt. 11:27; Mark 1:11; 9:7; 13:32; 14:36.
70. E.g., John 7:18; 8:46; 2 Cor. 5:21; 1 Peter 1:19; 2:22; 3:18; 1 John 3:5, 7.
71. Grant and Kitzinger, *Civilization of the Ancient Mediterranean*, 2:910–11.
72. Cf. Ex. 28:1; Lev. 8:1; Num. 16:5.
73. F. F. Bruce, "Melchizedek," *NBD*, 759.
74. Matt. 26:36–46; Mark 14:32–42; Luke 22:40–46.
75. Plutarch, *Alexander* 33.10; Philostratus, *De Gymnastica* 46.
76. Spicq, *TLNT*, 2:552–54.
77. E.g., Gal. 4:3, 9; Col. 2:8, 20; 2 Peter 3:10, 12.
78. Philo, *Prelim. Studies* 149–50.
79. Westcott, *Hebrews*, 134.
80. Epictetus, *Diss.* 2.16.39, 44.
81. Philo, *Agriculture* 9.
82. F. F. Bruce, *Hebrews*, 140.
83. Jacob Neusner and William Scott Green, eds., *Dictionary of Judaism in the Biblical Period: 450 B.C.E. to 600 C.E.* (New York: Simon and Schuster and Prentice Hall International, 1996), 2:526–27.
84. Spicq, *TLNT*, 3:477–78.
85. Grant and Kitzinger, *Civilization of the Ancient Mediterranean*, 2:963.
86. 1 Chron. 16:15; Ps. 105:8; 111:5.
87. Cf. Rom. 2:6–7; 1 Cor. 3:13–15; James 2:15– 16; 1 John 3:16–20.
88. E.g., 1 Cor. 11:1; Eph. 5:1; Phil. 3:17; 1 Thess. 1:6; 2:14.
89. Grant and Kitzinger, *Civilization of the Ancient Mediterranean*, 1:622.
90. Philo, *Dreams* 1.12.
91. Num. 35:9–34; Deut. 4:41–43; Josh. 20:1– 9.
92. Grant and Kitzinger, *Civilization of the Ancient Mediterranean*, 1:353.
93. Plutarch, *Moralia*, 446A.
94. Philo, *Sacrifices* 90.
95. J. A. Fitzmyer, "'Now This Melchizedek' (Heb. 7:1)," *CBQ* 25 (1963): 305–21.
96. Neusner and Green, eds., *Dictionary of Judaism in the Biblical Period*, 1:278–79.
97. Hurst, *The Epistle to the Hebrews*, 13.
98. J. A. Thompson, *The Book of Jeremiah* (NICOT; Grand Rapids, Mich.: Eerdmans, 1980), 551.
99. Neusner and Green, *Dictionary of Judaism in the Biblical Period*, 2:423.
100. F. B. Huey, *Bible Study Commentary: Exodus* (Grand Rapids, Mich.: Zondervan, 1977), 107.
101. Attridge, *Hebrews*, 184–85.
102. E.g., Ezek. 1:4–14; *1 En.* 61:10; 71:7.
103. Spicq, *TLNT*, 3:332–33.
104. *Dreams* 1.142–43; *Moses* 2.1.66.
105. E.g. Westcott, *Hebrews*, 266. For the correct interpretation see Alan M. Stibbs, *The Meaning of the Word "Blood" in Scripture* (reprint, Leicester, Eng.: Theological Students' Fellowship, 1978).
106. Spicq, *TLNT*, 3:344–50.
107. Plato, *Rep.* 7.514A–517A.
108. Cicero, *De off.* 3.17.69.
109. Attridge, *Hebrews*, 271.
110. Guthrie, *Hebrews*, 341.
111. Spicq, *TLNT*, 3:56–62.
112. As quoted in Attridge, *Hebrews*, 285.
113. E.g., Gal. 5:13; 1 Thess. 1:3; James 2:8; 1 Peter 1:22; 1 John 3:10–18; Rev. 2:19.
114. E.g., Isa. 2:2–21; Joel 1–3; Amos 8:9–11; 9:9–12.
115. E.g., *1 En.* 94:9; *4 Ezra* 7:26–44.
116. E.g., 1 Cor. 5:5; 1 Thess. 5:2; 2 Peter 3:10.

117. Michael R. Cosby, "The Rhetorical Composition of Hebrews 11," *JBL* 107 (1988): 250–70.
118. *Praem. poen.* 11–15.
119. Neusner and Green, eds., *Dictionary of Judaism in the Biblical Period*, 1:137.
120. Josephus, *Ant.* 1.3.2 §75.
121. E.g., *Jubilees* 10–12; *Apoc. Ab.* 1–8; *Gen. Rabbah* 38:13; Rom. 4:16–25; Gal. 3:6–14; 4:21–31.
122. Ellingworth, *Hebrews*, 594; see also 1 Peter 2:11.
123. Mary Rose D'Angelo, *Moses in the Letter to the Hebrews* (SBLDS; Chico, Calif.: Scholars, 1979), 91–131.
124. Bruce, *Hebrews*, 320.
125. On Jeremiah, who tradition says was stoned in Egypt, see Tertullian, *Scorpiace* 8; Jerome *Contra Jovinianum* 2:37. On the martyrdom of Isaiah see *Mart. Isa.* 5:11–14; Jutin, *Dial.*, 120; Jerome, *Comm. in Isa.*, 57:2.
126. See, e.g., 1 Cor. 9:24–27; Gal. 2:2; 2 Tim. 4:7; *4 Ezra* 7:127.
127. Philo, *Migration* 133.
128. Philo, *Agriculture* 119.
129. Attridge, *Hebrews*, 365.
130. Philo is typical of those who see Esau as a representative of wicked living. See. e.g., *De virtutibus* 208; *Legum allegoriae* 3.139–40.
131. Gen. 22:1–14; Ex. 3:1–2; Ezek. 28:13–15.
132. Leland Ryken et al., *DBI*, 573.
133. E.g., Ex. 19:16–22; 20:18–21; Deut. 4:11–12; 5:23–27.
134. Ezek. 46:11; Hos. 2:11; 9:5; Amos 5:21.
135. Ex. 19:18; Judg. 5:5; Ps. 68:8; 77:18.
136. 1 Cor. 7:31; 2 Peter 3:10–12; Rev. 21:1.
137. Rom. 12:10; 1 Thess. 4:9; 1 Peter 1:22; 2 Peter 1:7.
138. E.g., John 13:34–35; 1 Cor. 13:1, 13.
139. A. Berger, "Prison," *OCD*, 879.
140. As quoted in Harry T. Peck, *Harper's Dictionary of Classical Literature, and Antiquities* (New York: Harper & Brothers, 1898), 278.
141. Leon Morris, "Hebrews," *EBC*, 146.
142. E.g., Matt. 25:36; 1 Cor. 4:17–18; 2 Tim. 1:16; Heb. 13:18–19.
143. E.g. 1 Cor. 5:10–11; Eph. 4:19; 1 Thess. 4:3–6.
144. Lane, *Hebrews 9–13*, 533–35.
145. Westcott, *Hebrews*, 445.
146. D. F. Watson, "Letter, Letter Form," *DLNT*, 651.
147. Attridge, *Hebrews*, 404–5.
148. J. L. Wu, "Liturgical Elements," *DLNT*, 660.

Sidebar and Chart Notes
A-1. Ps. 97:7; 104:4; see Heb. 1:6–7.
A-2. Ps. 45:6–7; 102:25–27.
A-3. Spicq, *Theological Lexicon of the New Testament*, 3:344–46.
A-4. Leland Ryken et al., eds., *Dictionary of Biblical Imagery*, 752–54; e.g., Matt. 8:25; Mark 3:23–27; 5:28; James 5:15; Rom. 5:9–10; Rom. 2:5; 1 Thess. 2:16.
A-5. D'Angelo, *Moses*, 91–131.
A-6. Ex. 29:29–30; Lev. 16:32; Num. 18:7; 25:11–13; 35:25, 28; Neh. 12:10–11.
A-7. See esp. Philo, *Alleg. Interp.* 3.79–82.
A-8. Lane (*Hebrews 1–8*, 160–61) points out the differences between this conception of Melchizedek and that given by Hebrews.
A-9. For a detailed look at Melchizedek outside the biblical literature see Attridge, *Hebrews*, 192–95.
A-10. *4 Ezra* 7:26.
A-11. *2 Bar.* 59:4.
A-12. Josephus, *Ant.* 4.8.17–23 §§224–57.
A-13. Attridge, *Hebrews*, 311–14.
A-14. Philo, *Abraham* 270.
A-15. Grant and Kitzinger, eds., *Civilization of the Ancient Mediterranean*, 3:1359.
A-16. E.g. Prov. 13:24; Sir. 30:1.
A-17. See comments on Heb. 12:5–6; see also Deut. 8:5; Jer. 2:30; 5:3.
A-18. James 4:13; 1 Peter 4:9; Matt. 10:11; Acts 16:15; Titus 3:13; Philem. 22; 3 John 5–8.
A-19. As quoted in Spicq, *TLNT*, 3:455–56.

JAMES

by Douglas J. Moo

We meet several men in the New Testament who have the name James (see "Men Named 'James' in the New Testament"). Only two of them were prominent enough to write a letter to Christians and identify themselves simply as "James": James the brother of John, one of the twelve apostles; and James "the brother of the Lord." The former James, as Luke tells us, was executed by Herod Agrippa I in A.D. 44 (Acts 12:2); and this letter was probably not written this early. So we are left with James the brother of the Lord as the most likely author. This James did not at first believe in his brother's messianic claims (see John 7:5), but was apparently converted as a result of a resurrection appearance (cf. 1 Cor. 15:7). He became the leader of the early Christian church in Jerusalem.[1]

JORDAN NEAR
THE DEAD SEA
◀

▶ James
IMPORTANT FACTS:

- **AUTHOR:** James, the brother of the Lord.
- **DATE:** A.D. 44–48.
- **OCCASION:** James, leader of the Jerusalem church, writes to former parishioners who have had to leave Jerusalem to take up lives elsewhere.
- **THEMES:** The overall theme is expressed in 4:4–5: Believers must commit themselves wholeheartedly to their God, who demands absolute allegiance. Subordinate themes are:
  1. Encouragement for believers who are suffering trials.
  2. God's perspective on wealth and poverty.
  3. The need for biblical faith always to show itself in good works.

The New Testament tells us little about James's own background. Some Christians in the patristic period picture James as a radical Jewish-Christian who insisted on observance of Torah for Christians.[2] But the letter of James itself paints a different picture. To be sure, the letter is thoroughly Jewish—so Jewish that a few scholars have thought that it might be a Jewish book with the name of Jesus added later. But the Greek of the letter reveals that the author is well acquainted with good Greek style and with certain Greek religious and philosophical concepts. In fact, the letter uses words and concepts in ways similar to certain other Greek-influenced Jewish writings of the time: the book of Sirach, the *Testaments of the Twelve Patriarchs* in the Pseudepigrapha, and (less strikingly) the works of the Alexandrian philosopher Philo. We can surmise, therefore, that James, though raised in Galilee, had at some point become acquainted with the particular Hellenistic trajectory of Jewish moral thinking. God used that background to prepare him to write a letter of moral exhortation to struggling and tempted believers.

One other element in James's background deserves brief comment: his exact physical relationship to Jesus. Powerful ascetic tendencies in the church of the second and third centuries led to the view that Mary remained perpetually a virgin. New Testament references to "brothers" of the Lord constituted an obvious challenge to this view. Hence, Jerome and other fathers argued that the Greek word (*adelphos*) in these texts meant "cousin." But evidence for this meaning of the word in the New Testament is lacking. If James was an *adelphos* of the Lord, he and Jesus must have shared at least one blood parent. Some scholars think that this common parent was Joseph, and that James was older than Jesus, born to Joseph and a wife before Mary (this is called the Epiphanian view). But the close relationship between Mary and the brothers of Jesus (e.g., Mark 3:32; 6:3) suggests that Mary was the mother of Jesus' brothers also. In this case, James would have been a younger brother of Jesus (the so-called Helvidian view). If James was, then, born to the same parents as Jesus and raised in the same home, we may surmise that

Men Named "James" in the New Testament	
James, the father of Judas	• his son, Judas, was one of the twelve apostles • see Luke 6:16; Acts 1:13
James, the son of Alphaeus	• one of the twelve apostles • see Luke 6:15; Acts 1:13
James, the brother of John	• the son of Zebedee • one of the twelve apostles • killed by Herod Agrippa I (Acts 12:2) • see Luke 5:10; 9:28, 54; Acts 1:13
James, the brother of the Lord	• half-brother of the Lord Jesus; son of Mary and Joseph (cf. Mark 6:3) • see Acts 12:17; 15:13; 21:18; Gal. 1:19; 2:9, 12; 1 Cor. 15:7; letter of James; Jude 1

this background influenced his views of Christianity. In fact, however, we have little evidence that this was the case. Physical relationship to Jesus did not, apparently, lead to much spiritual benefit for James.[3]

The Recipients of the Letter

James describes the people he is writing to very generally: "the twelve tribes scattered among the nations" (1:1). "Twelve tribes" might suggest that James is writing to Jewish Christians, or even to Jews. But the language had become symbolic of the people of God and may have been transferred to Christians in general. Nevertheless, the content of the letter certainly suggests a Jewish-Christian audience.

Where did these Jewish Christians live? "Scattered among the nations" indicates that they were living outside of Palestine. The verb James uses here is cognate to the word "Diaspora," the name given to the Jewish community outside of Israel.

But since we think James is writing at an early date (A.D. 44–48), his recipients probably do not live far from Palestine. In fact, Acts 11:19 suggests the circumstances of the readers that James addresses in the letter: "Those who had been scattered by the persecution in connection with Stephen traveled as far as Phonecia, Cyprus and Antioch, telling the message only to Jews." On this scenario, then, the Jewish Christians James addresses are living as exiles in areas near Palestine because of their faith in Jesus. Their status as exiles explains why they are experiencing some of the trials James mentions. They are poor (cf. James 5:1–11), they are hauled into court by wealthy people (2:4–6), and they are oppressed by large landowners (5:5–6).

These are typical difficulties faced by exiles, accentuated in the case of these particular exiles by the hostility stemming from Jews who are unhappy with their commitment to Jesus as Messiah.

Some scholars are persuaded that this background data provides the key socioeconomic criterion by which James must be interpreted. Such interpreters think that James defends the poor, who are righteous, against the rich, who are evil. The letter of James has therefore become a favorite among liberation theologians.[4] But the situation in James is not as simple as that. The most natural interpretation of 1:10 suggests that there were "brothers" in the churches James addresses who were themselves rich. His reference to traveling business people in 4:13–17 suggests the same scenario. Ultimately, therefore, while James has a lot to say about poverty and wealth, we are prevented by the letter itself from any such simplistic equations as "rich=evil" or "poor=righteous." James's concern is not ultimately with economics or social status, although these play their role in the situation of the readers. His concern is with the spiritual problems created, in part, by these circumstances.

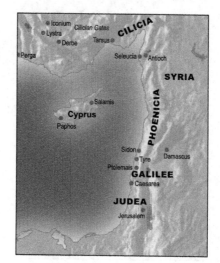

The Letter

James clearly belongs in the genre of *letter*. But on the wide spectrum of ancient letter types, it falls more toward the literary end than the personal end. Absent from James are the greetings, personal references, specific situations, and so on, that mark a more personal type of letter. The lack of these features, along with the vague address, has led some to categorize James as a *general* letter, written to the whole church rather than to a single church. But James has a definite audience in view; it is just that the audience is scattered across a large area and that he writes to that audience as a whole.

Other genres, or literary styles, are also thought to influence James. One of the most influential commentaries on James in the twentieth century was written by Martin Dibelius.[5] He argued that

▶

THE DISPERSION OF THE JEWS

The Jewish dispersion extended as far east as Media and Parthia and west to Italy and beyond.

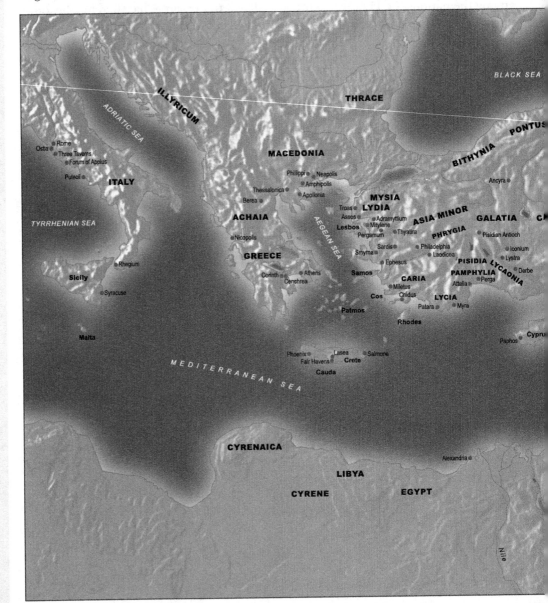

James belonged in the genre called *paraenesis*. This genre was characterized, according to Dibelius, by four features: (1) a focus on moral exhortation; (2) attention to a general rather than specific situations; (3) the use of traditional material; and (4) loose organization. Each of these characteristics is, indeed, typical of James—although most interpreters now find a lot more organization in James than Dibelius did. But modern scholars are less certain that *paraenesis* was an identifiable genre. The most we can say is that James makes some use of a paraenetic style.

A second genre in which many scholars place James is wisdom literature.[6] James refers to wisdom twice (1:5; 3:13–18), and the brief, direct, and practical admonitions of the letter remind us of the style of Proverbs and similar books from the intertestamental period (Sirach,

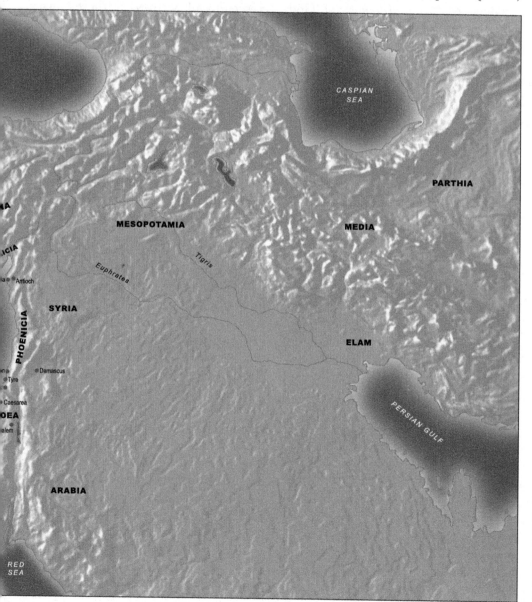

Wisdom of Solomon). However, James develops his topics at greater length than is typical of these books. The most we can say, again, is that James adopts certain conventions and emphases typical of wisdom books.

Introduction to the Letter (1:1)

James, a servant of God and of the Lord Jesus Christ (1:1). By calling himself a "servant" or "slave" (*doulos*) of God, James expresses his sense of being totally committed to the Lord. But the title also reveals his dignity, for it was used in the Old Testament of great leaders of Israel, such as Moses (Deut. 34:5; Dan. 9:11) and David (Jer. 33:21; Ezek. 37:25). James reveals his exalted view of Christ by associating him with God in this introduction to his letter.

To the twelve tribes scattered among the nations (1:1). Old Testament Israel, of course, was divided into twelve tribes, each headed by a patriarch, one of the sons of Jacob (or Israel). After the Israelites were "scattered among the nations" or "dispersed" in exile, hopes for a restoration of the nation were often expressed in terms of a reunification of the twelve tribes.[7] James is probably following the early Christian custom of referring to the church as the renewed Israel of the last days.

The Purpose and Benefit of Trials (1:2–12)

The topic of "trials" frames this section (1:2–4 and 1:12). James knows that his readers are experiencing tough times, including, as the letter indicates, poverty and persecution. So he begins by encouraging them to recognize that God has a purpose in trials: When we respond to them in wholehearted faith, they can bring us to a new level of spiritual maturity.

Consider it pure joy (1:2). James is not saying that we should pretend that trials are easy to take but that we should look beyond the difficulty to the spiritual benefit.

Because you know (1:3–4). The crescendo of virtues in these verses reminds us of two other passages in the New Testament where we find similar "stair-step" lists of virtues: Romans 5:3–4 and 2 Peter 1:5–7. These passages use an ancient literary device called *sorites*. The last virtue in the list is especially important, the goal toward which all the others lead. For James, this supreme virtue is being "mature and complete." Christian maturity is a big concern of James, a thread that runs through the fabric of his many exhortations.

If any of you lacks wisdom (1:5). Wisdom is a prominent idea in the Old Testament and in intertestamental Judaism. It is a practical idea: the ability to understand God's ways and to live in light of his purposes and values. James knows that genuine Christian maturity will be possible only if believers possess this wisdom from God.[8]

He must believe and not doubt (1:6–7). Since God is willing and able to give us the wisdom we need, any lack of wisdom must be our fault. The problem is that we do not always have the same kind of consistent attitude toward God that he has toward us. "Doubt" here refers to a conflict of loyalties that disturbs the purity of faith. James often refers to the teaching of Jesus in his letter, and he may be doing so here. For Jesus taught the disciples to expect answers to their prayers if they would only "have faith" and "not doubt" (Matt. 21:21).

A double-minded man (1:8). The word James uses here, *dipsychos*, means, literally, "double-souled." James may have been the first to use this word (see also 4:8), which expresses one of his central concerns. Hindering maturity in Christ, James suggests, is this fundamental duality in attitude and spirit. The importance of a single, focused affection for God is highlighted throughout the Old Testament, where sinners are described in terms similar to James as having a "divided heart."[9]

The brother in humble circumstances ... the one who is rich (1:9–10). The ancient world, like ours, featured great extremes of wealth and status. The problems that these conflicting situations in life created for Christians is an important theme in James. Many commentators think James here contrasts a Christian, who is poor (1:9), with a non-Christian, who is rich and arrogant (1:10–11). But the syntax suggests that the word "brother" in 1:9 should also be applied to the "one who is rich" in 1:10. On this reading, James is contrasting two kinds of Christians. Each kind of Christian, James suggests, has a particular kind of challenge, or "trial," to face. The poor Christian can become downhearted because of his or her low value on the world's socioeconomic scale. That Christian needs to rejoice in his or her identification with Christ, the "high position" he or she enjoys in Christ. But the rich Christian can become arrogant and self-satisfied. That kind of believer needs to remember that he or she is identified with one who is meek and lowly, despised by the world.

The rich man will fade away (1:11). On our reading of 1:9–10, these words refer not to condemnation at the judgment but to the transitory nature of all worldly wealth and status. The rich believer must remember that wealth cannot be brought into the eternal kingdom of Jesus Christ.

Blessed is the man who perseveres under trial (1:12). James wraps up this first paragraph of his letter by returning to where he began: trials. He encourages us to adopt the right attitude toward the problems that life brings our way by reminding us of the reward that God has for us when we "persevere," namely, "the crown of life."

The crown of life (1:12). The Greek word for "crown" here (*stephanos*) probably refers not to a royal crown but to the laurel wreath given to victorious athletes. Paul uses the word in just this way in 1 Corinthians 9:25: "Everyone who competes in the games goes into strict training.

REFLECTIONS

IN CALLING ON POOR CHRISTIANS TO BOAST IN THEIR exaltation with Christ and rich Christians to boast in their humility as they identify with Christ, James suggests that the church should be an institution in which the usual worldly markers of status are left behind. For in Christ all are equal—alike in needing to be saved by grace and alike in depending daily on that same grace for spiritual vigor and hope for the future. Yet the equality James pictures is often absent in the modern church. We fawn over the rich and powerful and ignore the poor and insignificant. We perpetuate the world's distinctions by the way we dress and the way we act. We need to work hard at becoming the kind of church that focuses only on spiritual distinctions.

They do it to get a crown that will not last; but we do it to get a crown that will last forever." Since James, like Paul, is thinking of a metaphorical crown, "life" is probably the reward denoted by the crown. A similar idea appears in Revelation 2:10, a word from Jesus to suffering Christians: "Be faithful, even to the point of death, and I will give you the crown of life."

Trials and Temptations (1:13–18)

The transition from 1:2–12 to 1:13–18 is easier to spot in Greek, because the word for "trial" and "temptation" is the same in Greek (*peirasmos*). But beyond the play on words, James undoubtedly sees an important connection in content. One of the gravest challenges Christians under trial face is temptation: temptation to question God's goodness or even his very existence. James therefore reminds us that, however difficult the circumstances, God is always working for our good.

DRAGGED AWAY

Net fishing in the Sea of Galilee.

▼

No one should say, "God is tempting me" (1:13). The Scriptures make clear that God does bring trials to his people, as

when he "tested" Abraham (Gen. 22:1). But God never "tempts" his people; he never entices them to commit an evil act. This whole issue of God's providence in trials was one that many Jews in the first century were debating.[10] Some were apparently excusing evil actions by claiming that God was himself leading them to do such acts. James does not want any of his readers to suffer under this blasphemous error. God, by his very nature, can never desire that his people sin.

Each one is tempted ... by his own evil desire (1:14). Temptation, James makes clear, comes not from God but from within, from each person's "evil desire." Here James may be reflecting Jewish teaching about conflicting "desires" within people. Some rabbis taught that each person has within him or her two "desires" or "tendencies": the *yetzer ha-ra*, "the tendency toward evil," and the *yetzer ha-tov*, "the tendency toward good."[11] Sin arises when the *yetzer ha-ra* drags away and entices people.

The language of "drag away" and "entice" reflects the activities of hunting and fishing: Like bait on a hook, sin tempts people and then drags them away. But the Jewish philosopher Philo had already used such language to describe the process of temptation: "There is no single thing that does not yield to the enticement of pleasure, and get caught and dragged along in her entangling nets."[12]

Desire ... gives birth to death (1:15). Switching metaphors, James now describes the continuing effects of sin in terms of conception. Temptation comes to all of us, but it is when we listen to the voice of desire that sin begins. If sin is not checked, it will ultimately result in eternal, spiritual death. Persevering under trials brings life (1:12), but succumbing to the temptation that accompanies trials brings death.

Every good and perfect gift is from above (1:17). To reinforce his teaching that God does not tempt people, James reminds us of what God does do: He gives his people good and perfect gifts. The Greek of 1:17 is carefully structured in an almost poetic rhythm, suggesting that James might be quoting from an early saying about God. Philo, for instance, makes a point similar to James, contrasting God's unchanging nature with the variations that are an inevitable part of the created world.[13]

The Father of the heavenly lights (1:17). "Heavenly lights" is a good interpretive rendering of the Greek, which has simply "lights." James is referring to the "lights" that appear in the sky: sun, moon, planets, stars (cf. Ps. 136:7–9; Jer. 31:35). "Father" connotes God's creative power. As the creator of the heavenly bodies, God, unlike them, is without change. Philo makes a similar point: "Every created thing must necessarily undergo change, for this is its property, even as unchangeableness is the property of God."[14]

He chose to give us birth through the word of truth (1:18). God's supreme gift to us is the new birth. In using this imagery, James both continues the metaphor of 1:15 and picks up a popular early Christian way of describing conversion. Jesus, of course, spoke of the need for such a new birth to Nicodemus (John 3:3); Peter also writes to Christians that "you have been born again, not of perishable seed, but of imperishable, through the living and enduring word of God" (1 Peter 1:23).

True Religion (1:19–27)

With this paragraph, James begins to develop one of his greatest themes: the indispensability of works for any genuine Christian experience. James develops this point in three paragraphs. In 1:19–27, he introduces it by contrasting true and false religion. In 2:1–13 he illustrates the point with reference to the issue of discrimination in the church. And in 2:14–26 he takes a more theological tack, showing that works are necessary to secure a positive verdict from God in the judgment.

Quick to listen, slow to speak and slow to become angry (1:19–20). These verses are a kind of "aside" in James's argument, not directly related to what came before or what comes after. Passages like this remind us of books like Proverbs, in which various topics are treated in quick succession. The theme of careful speech is also prominent in Proverbs. Jewish wisdom teaching stressed the importance of speaking deliberately and carefully.[15] These sources also connect looseness in speech with unrestrained anger, explaining James's quick move from speech to anger in these verses.

The righteous life that God desires (1:20). The NIV is an interpretive rendering of a Greek phrase that literally translated is "the righteousness of God." But the interpretation seems to be justified here, since the Old Testament and Jewish writers often used this language to describe the moral righteousness that met God's own standard of righteousness.[16]

Therefore . . . accept the word planted in you (1:21). With this verse, James turns to the key idea in this paragraph: the right response to God's word. "Accepting" the word often refers to conversion in the New Testament, but this meaning does not work here, where James is writing to Christians. Rather, "accepting" the word here means to allow it to have its intended impact on our lives. James has told us (1:18) that this word was used by God to bring us into his family. When that happens, he now notes, this word becomes "planted" in us. He probably is thinking of the famous prophecy of Jeremiah 31:31–34, where God promised to make a new covenant with his people and to write his law on the hearts of his people. Christians have God's word planted within them and now need to let it grow and flourish.

right ▶

BRONZE MIRROR
A mirror discovered in Canaanite excavations.

Do what it says (1:22). Lest we fail to understand what James means by "accepting" the word, he now spells it out: We must "do" it. People who only listen to the word are deceiving themselves, convinced that they are acceptable to God when they are not. This point is one that is made often by Jewish teachers also: "Not the expounding [of the law] is the chief thing, but the doing [of it]."[17]

Like a man who looks at his face in a mirror (1:23). James reinforces his point with an illustration. The "mirror" in the ancient world was composed of polished metal, usually bronze. How foolish it would be for a person to look at himself or herself in such a mirror and then do nothing about it—to see in a mirror that one's hair is all ahoo and not comb it afterwards! But just as foolish, James implies, are people who hear God's spoken message but then do nothing about it.

The man who looks intently into the perfect law . . . doing it . . . will be blessed (1:25). Some commentators think that the contrast between the man of 1:23–24 and the man of 1:25 is the intensity with which they look—an interpretation perhaps reflected in the NIV rendering "looks intently" in 1:25. But the contrast is probably simpler than that. The person in 1:25 is blessed for one reason: because, in contrast to the person described in 1:23–24, this person responds to what he or she sees or hears. It is the *doing* that brings blessing.

The sequence of words to describe the message of God in these verses is striking. James began with "the word of truth" as an instrument of conversion (1:18). Then he spoke of the importance of doing the "word" (1:22). Now he calls for Christians to look intently into, and respond to, "the perfect law that gives freedom." What James is implicitly saying is that God's word is one single entity, and we cannot pick and choose from it. If we want the benefit of the "gospel," the word that brings us into God's family, we must also respond to the "law," the word that commands and instructs us.

If anyone considers himself religious (1:26–27). The words "religion" and "religious" do not occur often in the New Testament. But they occur widely in the ancient Greek world, where they connote especially outward acts of worship. See, for instance, Philo's reference to "the worship of the gods in the different cities."[18] James perhaps uses the term here to reinforce his stress on outward works. He wants to leave no doubt about the practical nature of doing the word.

The "religion" God accepts will reveal itself in three activities: care in speech, concern for the helpless in society, and the avoidance of worldly attitudes and values. James has already mentioned care in speech (1:19), and he will return to the subject again (3:1–11). "Widows and orphans" are often singled out in the Old Testament as people of special concern to God (Ps. 68:5) and therefore as people who deserve kindness and help from God's people (cf. Isa. 1:10–17). Lest we think that doing the word involves only outward acts, James reminds us that obedience to God also includes and, indeed, is often the product of, an inner mind-set that avoids the contagion of the world's false ideas and values.

Condemnation of Discrimination (2:1–13)

James now applies the general principle of 1:19–27 to a specific situation. The person who is truly religious will not discriminate against the poor. For such discrimination violates the kingdom law of love. In other words, the person who discriminates is not doing the word.

Our glorious Lord Jesus Christ (2:1). This rendering, found in most English Bibles, is probably correct. But it is worth noting that the phrase could also be translated "our Lord Jesus Christ, the glorious one." The basis for this rendering is the Old Testament use of "glory" (Heb. *kabōd*) to signify God's own presence (cf. 1 Sam. 4:22). On this view, James is transferring the title "glory" to Jesus Christ.

Favoritism (2:1). The Greek word behind "favoritism" is, literally, "receiving the face" (*prosōpolēmpsia*). The word was apparently invented by the New Testament writers as a literal rendering of the Hebrew word for partiality.[19] "Receiving the face" vividly portrays the essence of partiality: making judgments about people on the basis of outward appearance.

Your meeting (2:2). The Greek word is *synagōgē*, which everywhere else in the New Testament refers to the Jewish house of study and worship. The Jewish Christians to whom James writes, then, may still be worshiping regularly in the synagogue. But the qualification "your" *synagōgē* may imply that the Christian believers are already gathering for worship in their own assembly (the word is used this way in Hermas, *Mandates* 11.9). Another possibility is that *synagōgē* refers more generally to a "meeting" or "gathering" of Christians to sit in judgment over a dispute between two believers. James uses a lot of judicial language in this context, and the situation he depicts in 2:2–3 is somewhat similar to community judicial settings described by the rabbis. See *b. Shebuot* 31a: "How do we know that, if two come to court, one clothed in rags and the other in fine raiment worth a hundred manehs, they should say to him, 'Either dress like him, or dress him like you'"; and *Sifre 4.4* (on Lev. 19:15): "You must not let one litigant speak as much as he wants, and then say to the other, 'Shorten thy speech.' You must not let one stand and the other sit."

Wearing a gold ring (2:2). The gold ring was an emblem of the upper-level Roman "equestrian" class.

Have you not discriminated among yourselves (2:4). These words can also be translated, "Are you not divided in yourselves?" The Greek verb James uses here (*diakrinō*) occurs in 1:6 with this sense of "doubt, be divided."[20] James's point may be, then, that the believers' discrimination against the poor is an indication of the deeply divided nature of their spiritual allegiance, which is at the heart of James's concern throughout the letter.

Listen, my dear brothers (2:5). The call to "listen" reminds us of similar appeals from the Old Testament; see, e.g., Deuteronomy 6:3: "Hear, O Israel, and be

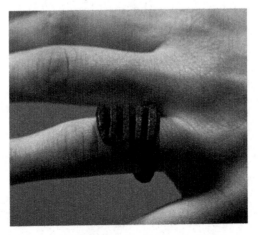

▶

RING

A key worn on the finger as a ring found in excavations of Herodian-era Jerusalem.

careful to obey so that it may go well with you and that you may increase greatly in a land flowing with milk and honey, just as the LORD, the God of your fathers, promised you."

Has not God chosen those who are poor in the eyes of the world to be rich in faith? (2:5). James's teaching about poverty and wealth can be accurately appraised only if we read what he says against the background of biblical teaching. In the Old Testament, the Hebrew word 'anaw (plural 'anawim) sometimes refers to people who are "poor" in a spiritual sense: humble and meek, recognizing their own weakness and utter dependence on God for deliverance.[21] It is this biblical usage of the word that explains the variation in Jesus' beatitude: "Blessed are you who are poor" (Luke 6:20) / "Blessed are the poor in spirit" (Matt. 5:3).

In James 2:5, the word "poor" has mainly an economic sense. James reminds his readers that God delights to choose those who are of no account in this world to inherit great blessing in the world to come. But the spiritual sense of the word is also hinted at. Indeed, James may well have in mind Jesus' beatitude as he writes, for he is permeated with influence from the teaching of Jesus.

Is it not the rich who are exploiting you? (2:6). James reflects accurately here (and in 5:1–6) the class divisions that wracked the first-century Middle East. Wealthy landholders were constantly increasing their land holdings at the expense of the poor. The poor, in turn, were forced to work for the rich on their own terms, a situation the rich took advantage of by suppressing wages and other unjust activities. Of course, such a situation was nothing new; the Old Testament prophets often denounced just such practices. See, for example, Amos 4:1: "Hear this word, you cows of Bashan on Mount Samaria, you women who oppress the poor and crush the needy and say to your husbands, 'Bring us some drinks!'"

The noble name of him to whom you belong (2:7). The NIV is a fair paraphrase of a cumbersome Greek construction, which, literally translated, reads: "the good name that has been called over you." The Greek itself is awkward because it is a rather literal translation of a Semitic phrase. To have a name "called" over one means to be owned by that person. A good example of this usage is found in Amos 9:12, which is quoted in Acts 15:17: "so that they may possess the remnant of Edom and all the nations that bear my name [lit., that are called by my name]."

The royal law found in Scripture (2:8). The NIV suggests that the love command from Leviticus 19:18 *is* the "royal law." But the preposition "in" can also be translated "according to" (Gk. *kata*), in which case James may be referring to a royal law that is based on, or similar to, Leviticus 19:18. That law may then be Jesus' own ratification of the love command. When asked what the greatest commandment was, Jesus cited the command to love God and love one's neighbor as oneself (cf. Matt. 22:34–40). On this interpretation the word "royal" means "coming from the king," a meaning well established in intertestamental Judaism. Philo, for instance, uses the same word James uses here (*basilikos*) to refer to the law of God, claiming that it is "royal" because it both belongs to God and leads to him.[22] Jesus established the law of love as a central demand of the kingdom he

inaugurated. It is to this "law" that James probably refers.

Love your neighbor as yourself (2:8). James quotes Leviticus 19:18 because Jesus himself highlighted this command as basic to God's moral demand. But its appropriateness in this context is accentuated by the fact that a prohibition of partiality occurs in this same context (19:15). Indeed, James appears to mine the immediate context of 19:18 for a number of key moral exhortations that he passes on to his readers.[23]

Whoever keeps the whole law (2:10). The conviction that the law is a unity and that a person is therefore obliged to keep every part of it without exception was commonplace in James's day. The Stoics in particular emphasized the unity of vices and virtues. Augustine reflects this attitude: "Whoever has one virtue has all of them, and whoever does not have a particular one has none."[24] Jewish teachers claimed the same is true of God's law. For instance, when the pious Eleazar is commanded by a pagan king to eat forbidden food, he responds: "Do not suppose that it would be a petty sin if we were to eat defiling food; to transgress the law in matters either small or great is of equal seriousness, for in either case the law is equally despised" (*4 Macc.* 5:19–21).[25] Paul reflects the same strand of teaching in Galatians 5:3: "I declare to every man who lets himself be circumcised that he is obligated to obey the whole law." But critical for James, as usually is the case, may be Jesus' affirmation of the continuing relevance of every detail of the law:

I tell you the truth, until heaven and earth disappear, not the smallest letter, not the least stroke of a pen, will by any means disappear from the Law until everything is accomplished. Anyone who breaks one of the least of these commandments and teaches others to do the same will be called least in the kingdom of heaven, but whoever practices and teaches these commands will be called great in the kingdom of heaven. (Matt. 5:18–19)

"Do not commit adultery" . . . "Do not commit murder" (2:11). The order of the commandments does not, of course, follow the order of the commandments in their original context (Ex. 20:13–14; Deut. 5:17–18). But this order is found in one important manuscript of the LXX.[26]

Judgment without mercy will be shown to anyone who has not been merciful (2:13). The importance of mercy is highlighted in many Old Testament passages. Particularly noteworthy, because of the

connection between mercy and concern for the poor and powerless, is Zechariah 7:9–10: "This is what the LORD Almighty says: 'Administer true justice; show mercy and compassion to one another. Do not oppress the widow or the fatherless, the alien or the poor. In your hearts do not think evil of each other.'" See also *Testament of Zebulun* 8:1: "You also, my children, have compassion toward every person with mercy, in order that the Lord may be compassionate and merciful to you." Closest to home is Jesus' own promise: "Blessed are the merciful, for they will be shown mercy" (Matt. 5:7; cf. 18:21–35).

True Religion Manifested in Works (2:14–26)

James has insisted that our actions (mercy) will be taken into account in the judgment (2:12–13). But he has no wish to minimize the importance of faith. Thus, he argues that an unbreakable connection exists between saving faith and works.

Such faith (2:14). The NIV recognizes the importance of the article before the word "faith" in Greek by translating "such." This is vitally important. James is not contesting the saving ability of true faith; he claims that the faith "a man claims to have" but is without "deeds" cannot save.

If one of you says to him, "Go, I wish you well" (2:16). The pious wish expressed by the person claiming to have faith echoes a common biblical blessing. The Greek is more literally translated, "Depart in peace"; similar language occurs in both the Old Testament and New Testament.[27]

Faith by itself (2:17). A better rendering might be "in itself." What James is argu-

R E F L E C T I O N S

WHAT JAMES SAYS IN 2:8–13 MAY SEEM TO IMPLY that believers continue to be obliged to keep every single Old Testament commandment, including those pertaining to food, sacrifices, and civil affairs. But James hints at a broader perspective. He calls the law Christians are to obey the "royal law" (2:8), a reference, we have argued, to the law of the kingdom established by Jesus. He also calls it a "law that gives freedom," again suggesting that more than the Old Testament law itself may be in mind. In fact, we think James shares the perspective of Jesus, who both affirms the permanent validity of the Old Testament law and claims to be the One who now, as its fulfiller (Matt. 5:17), has the right to determine what its ultimate meaning and application are. In other words, James is not insisting that we will be judged by the law of the Old Testament but by the law, based on the Old Testament, set down by Jesus for our guidance.

▶ Was James Writing Against Paul's Teaching on Justification By Faith Alone?

Just why James puts so much emphasis on the relationship between faith and works is not certain. But one likely historical scenario goes like this. After his conversion, Paul preached in Damascus, Jerusalem (briefly), and in Tarsus (from perhaps about A.D. 36–45). Certainly during this time he would have developed his characteristic emphasis on faith alone as a means of justification. But Paul used justification in a peculiarly Christian sense, not always recognized by his opponents or his listeners.

We can surmise that Paul's emphasis has been misunderstood by some who have heard him preach and turned the doctrine into an excuse for not bothering any more with "works." James hears of this perverted form of Paul's teaching and attacks it in these verses. So we do not have to assume that James is directly attacking Paul. They have probably not yet had opportunity to learn about each other's theology; and, when they did, shortly after this at the Jerusalem Council (Acts 15), they would have had ample time to compare notes on this matter.

ing is that a faith unaccompanied by deeds is intrinsically unable to save. James's wording (*kath' heautēn*) has a parallel in a statement about the law in Josephus: "The greatest miracle of all is that our Law holds out no seductive bait of sensual pleasure, but has exercised this influence *through its own inherent merits.*"[28]

But someone will say (2:18). The sequence of thought in 2:18–19 is difficult to unravel. Who is James quoting? Is the person arguing against James or is he an ally of James? One factor in answering these questions is the literary background of the language James uses. He is employing at this point an ancient style called the "diatribe," which features a lively question-and-answer format to convince people of a certain viewpoint (see comments on this style in the introduction to Romans). The opening phrase "but someone will say" reflects this style and makes it quite certain that the person James is quoting is an opponent

rather than an ally. The closest New Testament parallel comes in 1 Corinthians 15:35: "But someone may ask, 'How are the dead raised?'"

You believe that there is one God (2:19). The monotheism maintained by these people who have faith without deeds is perhaps the most fundamental of all Jewish beliefs. It is enshrined in the *Shema*, a standard Jewish confession based on Deuteronomy 6:4: "Hear, O Israel: The LORD our God, the LORD is one" (it is called the *Shema* after the first Heb. word, "Hear"). The early Christians took over without question this Jewish monotheism.[29] James has no problem with this verbal profession; he is concerned that it is no more than an intellectual assent.

The demons believe that—and shudder (2:19). The Greek verb behind "shudder" (*phrissō*) occurs only here in the New Testament. But it is used in the papyri to describe the effect that a sorcerer aims to produce in his hearers.[30] Ancient people often thought that pronouncing a god's name had power to provoke fear and terror. Moreover, Philo uses this verb to describe the dread experienced by sinful people who know they deserve judgment.[31] James may then also be suggesting that the demons shudder in fear and trembling, recognizing in this truth about God the doom to which they are destined. In this respect the demons are better off than the so-called Christians James is attacking, for at least the demons have *some* reaction to their "orthodox" confession!

Our ancestor Abraham (2:21). James's appeal to Abraham as a key test case for

▶
A SORCERER'S PAPYRUS

A third-century magical text (*PGM* LXX).

his insistence on a faith that works is entirely natural. For it was God's promise to Abraham that formed the starting point for God's creation of his own people, Israel. "Descendants of Abraham" became a standard designation of God's people.[32]

Considered righteous (2:21). This expression translates one Greek verb (*dikaioō*, "to justify"). One key in reconciling the teaching of James and Paul on this matter is to recognize that they use this verb in different ways (see "Two Ways of Understanding 'Justify': Paul and James").

When he offered his son Isaac on the altar (2:21). Abraham was celebrated in Jewish tradition for his great moral virtue. "Abraham was perfect in all his deeds with the Lord, and well-pleasing in righteousness all the days of his life" (*Jub.* 23:10); Abraham "did not sin against thee" (Pr. Man. 8); "no one has been found like him in glory" (Sir. 44:19). Abraham's willingness to sacrifice his son Isaac (Gen. 22) is naturally highlighted as the pinnacle of his devout obedience. Philo claims that Abraham's offering of Isaac was the greatest of Abraham's "works" (*Abraham* 167).

▶ Two Ways of Understanding "Justify": Paul and James

Paul, in a creative move borne of his Christian convictions, uses the verb *dikaioō* ("to justify") to refer to the establishment of a right relationship with God in this life. But this was not the typical Old Testament and Jewish meaning of the verb. "Justification" usually referred to the ultimate verdict of God over a person in the time of judgment.[A-1] Jesus' own words express this perspective clearly: "By your words you will be acquitted [*dikaioō*], and by your words you will be condemned" (Matt. 12:37).

James, therefore, uses the language of justification in the typical Old Testament/Jewish manner to refer to what we would call the judgment. Against those who are suggesting that a person can be saved by faith apart from deeds, James cites Abraham to show that true faith is always revealed in deeds, and that these deeds are taken into consideration by God in the judgment.

Even more pertinent is the tradition reflected in 1 Maccabees 2:51–52: "Remember the deeds of the ancestors, which they did in their generations; and you will receive great honor and an everlasting name. Was not Abraham found faithful when tested, and it was reckoned to him as righteousness?" "When tested" almost certainly refers to the offering of Isaac, and the author of 1 Maccabees uses the language of Genesis 15:6 ("reckoned to him as righteousness") to interpret the significance of that event. This, of course, is precisely the text James quotes in 2:23. Paul also uses this text, but to make a different point.

Abraham believed God (2:23). James may be reacting also against some Jewish interpreters who viewed Abraham's faith in more or less intellectual terms, as his turning from idolatry to worship of the one God.[33]

God's friend (2:23). The Old Testament never uses this exact language about Abraham, although a few texts come close (cf. 2 Chron. 20:7; Isa. 41:8).[34] But Abraham was called the "friend of God" in Jewish tradition.[35]

Rahab the prostitute (2:25). Why does James choose the examples of Abraham and Rahab to illustrate his point about faith and works? Perhaps simply because they represent polar opposites: the patriarch and the prostitute, the revered founder of the Israelite nation and the pagan, immoral woman. But some scholars note a tradition that surfaces in the early Christian book *1 Clement*. In this book, Abraham and Rahab are cited together as examples of hospitality—Rahab, of course, because she welcomed and hid the Jewish spies and Abraham

because he received the three "men" who brought him news of God's promise (Gen. 18).[36] But it is not clear that his tradition predates James; and he makes no point of hospitality in this context.

Controlling the Tongue (3:1–12)

Having shown that "true religion" is rooted in a faith that infallibly produces works, James now turns to some of those deeds that believers particularly need to exhibit. The first of these is the control of one's speech. James echoes Old Testament wisdom teaching in his concern about personal speech habits. Our speech, James makes clear, reveals the attitude of the heart. A "divided" heart will lead to inconsistent habits of speech, while the person with a wholehearted allegiance to the Lord will be marked by godliness in speech.

If anyone is never at fault in what he says, he is a perfect man (3:2). The tongue, James argues here, is one of the hardest of all parts of the body to bring into full subjection to the Lord. The difficulty of avoiding sins of speech is acknowledged by Jewish authors who have apparently influenced James. Note, for example, Sirach 19:16: "A person may make a slip without intending it. Who has never sinned with his tongue?" See also Philo: "But if a man succeeded, as if handling a lyre, in bringing all the notes of the thing that is good into tune, bringing speech into harmony with intent, and intent with deed, such a one would be considered perfect and of a truly harmonious character."[37]

When we put bits into the mouths of horses to make them obey us, we can turn the whole animal (3:3). Appeal to

▶

HORSE'S BIT

A decorated horse
bit from the
ancient Near East.

a horse to illustrate how a small object can control a large one was widespread in the ancient world. The fifth-century B.C. playwright Sophocles has one of his characters say, "I know that spirited horses are broken by the use of a small bit."[38]

Or take ships as an example (3:4). James adds a second illustration of the way in which a small object controls a much larger one. Great ships, driven by strong winds, are steered by a relatively small rudder. This imagery is again common in James's day. Aristotle contrasted the small size of the rudder with the "huge mass" of the ship it controls.[39] But especially helpful in illuminating James are ancient texts that use the same combination of images found in these verses. A number of ancient writers, for instance, compare the rule of God over the world to the charioteer's guidance of the horse by reins and bit and to the pilot's steering of a ship.[40] We also find texts that combine references to charioteer, helmsman, and the taming of the animal world (cf. 3:7).[41] The best example comes from Philo:

> Mind is superior to Sense-perception. When the charioteer is in command and guides the horses with the reins, the chariot goes the way he

wishes. . . . A ship, again, keeps to her straight course, when the helmsman grasping the tiller steers accordingly. . . . Just so, when Mind, the charioteer or helmsman of the soul, rules the whole living being as a governor does a city, the life holds a straight course. . . . But when irrational sense gains the chief place . . . the mind is set on fire and is all ablaze, and that fire is kindled by the objects of sense which Sense-perception supplies.[42]

The moralist Plutarch even uses the imagery of a runaway ship and a fire to illustrate the destructive nature of loose speech. What these parallels reveal is that James is tapping into a widespread series of images from his culture to get his points across to his Christian readers.

Consider what a great forest is set on fire by a small spark (3:5). The Old Testament and Jewish authors had applied the imagery of the destructive and rapid spread of a fire to the damage caused by unrestrained speech. See, for example, Proverbs 16:27: "A scoundrel plots evil, and his speech is like a scorching fire"; Sirach 28:22: ["The tongue] has no power over the godly; they will not be burned in its flame."

The Greek word behind the NIV's "forest" is *hylē*, which means "wood." Forests being somewhat rare in the Middle East of James's day, the word may here refer to the brush on the hillsides of Palestine—easily consumed by fire in hot, dry weather.[43]

Is itself set on fire by hell (3:6). "Hell" translates the Greek *gehenna*, a transliteration of a Hebrew phrase that means "Valley of Hinnom." This valley, just outside of Jerusalem, had an evil reputation because trash was burned in it and pagan child sacrifices had been carried out there in earlier times (cf. Jer. 32:35). James again reveals his dependence on the teaching of Jesus, because this word occurs elsewhere in the New Testament only on his lips.

All kinds of animals, birds, reptiles and creatures of the sea (3:7). Although the words are not identical, James's reference to the creation account of Genesis 1 cannot be missed. See, for example, Genesis 1:26: "Then God said, 'Let us make man in our image, in our likeness, and let them rule over the fish of the sea and the birds of the air, over the livestock, over all the earth, and over all the creatures that move along the ground.'" Jewish and Christian writers reflect this same tradition.[44]

A restless evil (3:8). James has described the "double-minded" man as "unstable" in 1:8 (same Gk. word as translated "restless" here). This word was also occasionally applied to the tongue.[45]

Men, who have been made in God's likeness (3:9). Cursing other people is all the more terrible because these people bear God's own likeness. James again alludes to the creation account and is probably reflecting common Jewish teaching. The rabbis, for instance, taught that one should not say, "'Let my neighbor be put to shame'—for then you put to shame one who is in the image of God."[46]

My brothers, this should not be (3:10). James here rebukes Christians whose use of the tongue is "double"—blessing or praising God and cursing other human beings—acting unnaturally like a spring that gives forth both fresh and salty water (3:11). Certain Jewish moral teachings that James seems to know well emphasize the same problem of "doubleness" with the tongue. See, for instance, *Testament of Benjamin* 6:5: "The good set of mind does not talk from both sides of its mouth: praises and curses, abuse and honor, calm and strife, hypocrisy and truth, poverty and wealth, but it has one disposition, uncontaminated and pure, towards all men." Sirach 6:1 condemns "the double-tongued sinner."

Can a fig tree bear olives, or a grapevine bear figs? (3:12). The commonplace truth of the natural world, that plants bear according to their kind, was often

GRAPE VINES
AND A BRANCH
WITH FIGS
▼

employed in the ancient world to illustrate consistency. Epictetus, a second-century writer, asked, "How can a vine be moved to act, not like a vine, but like an olive, or again an olive to act, not like an olive, but like a vine? It is impossible, inconceivable."[47]

Peaceful Relations Through Wisdom (3:13–4:3)

Most Bibles and commentaries divide these verses into two separate paragraphs, but they have a lot in common. Both focus on the need for community reconciliation and make clear that such peace is the product only of the right mind-set.

Let him show it by his good life (3:13). James's insistence that wisdom is revealed in a godly lifestyle picks up a key theme of the letter (see 2:14–26) and reflects the common Jewish focus on the practical dimensions of wisdom. Wisdom, Proverbs reminds us, leads us to "walk in the ways of good men and keep to the paths of the righteous" (Prov. 2:20).

Selfish ambition (3:14). The sense of the word James uses here (*eritheia*) can be gleaned from its one pre-New Testament occurrence, in Aristotle, where it refers to the selfish party spirit that governed too many politicians in his day.[48]

Wisdom . . . is . . . peace-loving (3:17). In a text that reminds us of Paul's famous "fruit of the Spirit" passage, James lists the fruit of wisdom. Outstanding among this fruit is peace, which James emphasizes again in 3:18. Proverbs had already made the connection between wisdom and peace: "Her [wisdom's] ways are pleasant ways, and all her paths are peace" (Prov. 3:17).

Fights and quarrels (4:1). The Greek word behind "quarrels" (*machai*) means "battles" or "strife" of any kind. When we add the evidence of 4:2, where James refers to "killing," therefore, we may conclude that James is rebuking believers for engaging in violence of some kind in these verses. While at first sight it might seem impossible that Christians would be engaged in such violence with one

▶ First-Century Jewish Moral Teaching

The ideas found in these verses are also found together in several writings from the time of James. The best examples come from the intertestamental Jewish book *The Testaments of the Twelve Patriarchs*. Modeled on the speech of the dying Jacob to his twelve sons from Genesis 48–49, this book contains a "testament" from each of the twelve patriarchs to his children. In each testament, the patriarch recounts some of the key experiences of his life and uses them as a basis for moral instruction. The book was probably written in Greek sometime in the second century B.C., although it is widely thought that Christian scribes may have added

some material to the book as it was transmitted over time. The book has never been accepted as canonical by any part of the Christian church and appears in the collection called the "Pseudepigrapha."[A-2]

This book traces slander (*katalalia*, T. Gad 3:3), violence (*polemos*), and murder (T. Sim. 4:5) to jealousy. It also frequently condemns "double-mindedness." These are the themes that bind together James's argument in this part of the book. He is therefore adapting a literary theme about jealousy and its terrible effects that was apparently well known in certain Hellenistic Jewish circles.[A-3]

REFLECTIONS

JAMES IS NOT EXPLICITLY ADDRESS-ing church leaders in this paragraph. But he has mentioned "teachers" in 3:1, and especially prominent Christians may tend to think of themselves as "wise and understanding" (3:13). Leadership of God's church requires many gifts, some of them intellectual in nature. But the leader who brings lasting good to the church, fostering unity rather than division, will above all possess wisdom and the humility that comes from true biblical wisdom. Too many leaders are motivated, perhaps unconsciously, by the "party spirit" that is the mark of the wrong kind of wisdom (3:16). They make the mistake of confusing their own agendas with God's. The wise leader will have the humility to see the difference.

another (cf. "among you" in 4:1), certain elements in the religious and political atmosphere of the mid-first century make it at least possible, for the Jewish Zealot movement was becoming prominent at just this time.

This movement advocated violence in defense of Israel's right to be a theocracy. Some of the believers to whom James writes have been (former) Zealots and so brought their violence in defense of God and his kingdom into the church.[49] But surely James would have said more about the matter if the Christians are actually resorting to such violence. The words James uses in 4:1 are commonly applied to verbal "battles." Particularly applicable, in light of James's concern with speech in the context, is *Psalms of Solomon* 12:3, which warns that slanderous lips "kindle strife" (*polemos*, the word translated "fights" in 4:1).

They come from your desires (4:1). Behind the NIV "desires" is the Greek *hē-donē*, "pleasure." This word often refers to an attitude of sinful self-indulgence; we get our word "hedonistic" from it. James is not the first to trace sinful conduct to sinful desire; note, for instance, *4 Maccabees* 1:25–27: "In pleasure [*hē-donē*] there exists even a malevolent tendency, which is the most complex of all the emotions. In the soul it is boastfulness, covetousness, thirst for honor, rivalry, and malice; in the body, indiscriminate eating, gluttony, and solitary gormandizing."

You want something but don't get it. You kill and covet, but you cannot have what you want. You quarrel and fight (4:2). English versions differ over the punctuation of this verse (the original manuscripts, for the most part, had no punctuation). But the background of James's teaching strongly points to a punctuation different from what the NIV adopts. We may set it out as follows:

> You want something but you can't get it; so you kill.
> You covet and you cannot have what you want; so you quarrel and fight.

This arrangement preserves the parallelism of the verse. In each sentence, frustrated desire leads to a violent attitude. This is just the sequence we find in the theme about "envy" or "jealousy" that James depends on in these verses (see the introduction to 3:13–4:3). An excellent example is the *Testament of Simeon*. A substantial portion of this book deals with the problem of envy and describes how it led Simeon to seize and attempt to murder his brother Joseph. Simeon is portrayed as reflecting on his motivations and attitudes. He says, "Envy dominates the whole of man's mind" and "keeps prodding him to destroy the one whom he envies" (*T. Sim.* 3:2–3). A similar connection between envy and violence is implied by Epictetus, who notes that Caesar can free people from "wars and fightings" but not from "envy."[50] "Kill," then, is probably James's way of warning his readers about the ultimate outcome of the attitude they have adopted.

A Call to Wholehearted Commitment (4:4–10)

This paragraph is the heart of James's letter. In it he brings to a climax the underlying theme of the letter: the need for wholehearted, unreserved allegiance to God.

You adulterous people (4:4). The Greek is actually feminine: you "adulteresses." The use of the feminine form reinforces the biblical imagery that James depends on here. The Old Testament frequently portrays the relationship between God and his people in terms of marriage. See, for instance, Isaiah 54:4–6:

> "*Do not be afraid; you will not suffer shame.*
> *Do not fear disgrace; you will not be humiliated.*
> *You will forget the shame of your youth*
> *and remember no more the reproach of your widowhood.*
> *For your Maker is your husband—*
> *the LORD Almighty is his name—*
> *the Holy One of Israel is your Redeemer;*
> *he is called the God of all the earth.*
> *The LORD will call you back*
> *as if you were a wife deserted and distressed in spirit—*

> *a wife who married young,*
> *only to be rejected," says your God.*

This text is typical of Old Testament texts presenting the Lord as the husband and his people as the bride. When his people go astray after other gods, they can be said to be committing adultery against the Lord. Jeremiah compares unfaithful Israel to "a woman unfaithful to her husband" (Jer. 3:20). But the climax of this imagery comes in Hosea, who is commanded by the Lord to marry a faithless prostitute to illustrate the spiritual waywardness of Israel. In this abrupt and startling address of his readers, therefore, James reminds them of this broad biblical teaching about God's demand for unswerving faithfulness in his people's relationship to him.

REFLECTIONS

JAMES'S USE OF THE OLD TESTAMENT marital imagery to depict the relationship between the Lord and his people is vivid and convicting. As a jealous lover, God demands that we return to him an exclusive and unwavering love. No flirtation with the world is to be tolerated. Our allegiance to God must be wholehearted and consistent. This call for spiritual "oneness" lies at the heart of James's message to us today. The opposite of this "oneness" is the double-mindedness that he condemns in 1:8 and 4:8—thinking we can be friends with the world and be committed believers at the same time (see 4:4). James's strong and eloquent plea should stimulate each of us to look carefully at ourselves, seeking to uncover any hint of love for the world that is competing with our love for God.

Or do you think Scripture says without reason that the spirit he caused to live in us envies intensely? (4:5). Interpreters go in two radically different directions in this verse. The NIV represents one alternative: James reminds his readers that the Scripture itself warns about a proneness to sinful envy in the human spirit. But note the translation in the NIV note: "God jealously longs for the spirit that he made to live in us." This interpretation assumes that James is reminding his readers of the Old Testament emphasis on God's jealousy for his people.

Each interpretation fits well in the context, with its focus on both human envy (3:16; 4:2) and on God's demand for total allegiance from his people (4:4). But the latter theme is both closer in context and more striking. A reminder of God's jealousy for his people fits nicely in a context where James uses the imagery of faithfulness in marriage to make a spiritual point. If, then, we adopt the NIV alternative rendering, what is the "Scripture" to which James refers? A few interpreters think James may be referring to a noncanonical source, such as the *Apocalypse of Moses* or the lost *Book of Eldad and Modad*. But a more likely reference is the general Old Testament teaching about God's jealousy.[51] The singular "Scripture" (*graphē*) can sometimes refer in this manner to the Old Testament in general (cf. John 7:37–39).

God opposes the proud but gives grace to the humble (4:6). With this quotation of Proverbs 3:34, James sets the agenda for the next verses, in which he calls on his readers to humble themselves so that they can experience God's grace to them. Peter quotes this same text in a similar context in his first letter (1 Peter 5:5), one of the many points of contact between the letters. Probably both James and Peter rely on widespread early Christian moral tradition.

Come near to God and he will come near to you (4:8). The language of "come near" often refers to worship.[52] But this meaning does not fit this verse well, since it promises that God will also "come near" us. Probably, then, James uses the verb in a way similar to Hosea 12:6: "But you must return to your God; maintain love and justice, and wait for [LXX *engize*, come near] your God always." See also *Testament of Dan* 6:2, where the command to "draw near to God" is preceded by the exhortation to "be on your guard against Satan and his spirits" (cf. James 4:7).

Wash your hands, you sinners, and purify your hearts, you double-minded (4:8). James calls on his readers to transform both their outward behavior ("hands") and their inner attitude ("hearts"). The combination of "washing" and "purifying" stems from Old Testament requirements for priestly purity when administering the things of the Lord. The verbs have this sense the three times they occur together in the Old Testament.[53] Note also Psalm 24:3–4, which requires "clean hands and a pure heart" for those who would stand before the Lord.

Grieve, mourn and wail (4:9). James shifts from priestly to prophetic imagery. "Grieve," "mourn," and "wail" are all verbs used by the prophets to connote the radical and heartfelt repentance from sin that God calls for from his people. Joel, warning of the imminent Day of the Lord, pictures the Lord's inviting his people to "return to me with all your heart, with fasting and weeping and mourning" (Joel 2:12).

Change your laughter to mourning (4:9). James is no killjoy, wanting Christians to walk around with long faces and somber expressions. Key to understanding his exhortation here is to recognize that "laughter" is often associated with the "fool" in biblical wisdom. This is the person who scorns the Lord and any moral standards, delighting in sinful behavior and mocking any idea of judgment to come.[54] Jesus reflects this same tradition when he said, "Woe to you who laugh now, for you will mourn and weep" (Luke 6:25b).

Condemnation of Critical Speech (4:11–12)

In these verses James returns briefly to the theme of 3:1–12: the danger of sinful speech. He again reflects the moral theme that lies behind much of his teaching in chapters 3–4, for this theme

frequently linked "speaking evil" to jealousy, selfishness, quarrels, and pride.[55] The early Christian writer Hermas even claims that evil speech is the product of "double-mindedness."[56]

Anyone who speaks against his brother or judges him speaks against the law and judges it (4:11). James's reference to the "neighbor" in 4:12 suggests that the "law" he has in mind is again the love command—that is, Leviticus 19:18 (see James 2:8). The likelihood of this allusion is heightened when we note that Leviticus 19:16 prohibits slander. James may again be raising issues that are prominent in the Old Testament passage where the love command is given.

Condemnation of Arrogant Planning (4:13–17)

This paragraph and the next (5:1–6) resemble each other. Each begins with the formula "now listen" and each focuses on sins having to do with wealth.

▶

RELIEF OF A BATTLE SCENE

Trajan's column in Rome decorated with a spiral of series of battle reliefs.

The people James chastises in this paragraph appear to be well-to-do merchants who can afford to travel and look forward to earning a healthy profit. Some interpreters think these people might be non-Christians. But James's call on them to acknowledge the will of the Lord in what they do (4:15) suggests rather that they are believers who are becoming too self-sufficient and proud.

Now listen, you who say (4:13). This form of address is typical of the diatribe style James uses elsewhere in the letter (see comments on 2:18–21).

We will go to this or that city, spend a year there, carry on business and make money (4:13). The picture James paints with these words would have been familiar to his first-century readers. The first century was marked by growing commercial activity, which was especially true in the Hellenistic cities of Palestine (such as those in the Decapolis). Jews were especially prominent in these commercial ventures; many left Palestine to pursue their business interests.

You are a mist that appears for a little while and then vanishes (4:14). The Old Testament and Jewish literature is permeated with reminders of the transitory nature of human life. Proverbs 27:1 warns, "Do not boast about tomorrow, for you do not know what a day may bring forth." Life is compared to a "breath" in Job 7:7, 9; Psalm 39:5–6.

Anyone, then, who knows the good he ought to do and doesn't do it, sins (4:17). This reminder about "sins of omission" comes somewhat unexpectedly at the end of this paragraph. One commentator suggests, however, that

James may be including this saying because of some Old Testament texts that he had in mind. Proverbs 3:27–28 prohibits any delay in doing good to a neighbor; and in the LXX this prohibition is grounded in the warning that "you do not know what the next day will bring forth." James has already quoted from Proverbs 3 in James 4:6, so his attention may still be on this passage.[57]

Condemnation of the Wicked Rich (5:1–6)

The "rich people" that James addresses in this paragraph are not Christians. They manifest a selfish lifestyle inconsistent with Christian values, and James holds out no hope for their repentance. He simply condemns them. James thus imitates the prophets, who often pronounced doom on sinful pagan nations in prophecies directed to Israel. Their purpose is to reveal the seriousness of sin and to encourage the people of God who suffer from such sin to endure until the certain Day of Judgment to come.

You rich people (5:1). James can simply address these people as "rich" without explicitly saying that they are the "wicked" rich because of the biblical and Jewish tradition that tends to associate the rich and the wicked. "Rich" is sometimes a synonym for "the unrighteous" (e.g., Prov. 10:15–16; 14:20); and both Old Testament prophets and intertestamental Jewish writers regularly denounce the rich for their luxurious lifestyles and oppression of the poor.[58]

Weep and wail (5:1). Both these words (*klaiō* and *ololyzō*) occur frequently in the prophets to depict the reaction of wicked people when they are faced with the judgment of the Day of the Lord. See, for instance, Isaiah 13:6: "Wail, for the day of the LORD is near; it will come like destruction from the Almighty" (see also Isa. 15:3; Amos 8:3). The "misery" that is coming to the rich, therefore, is not earthly disaster but divine judgment.

Your wealth has rotted (5:2). Not all forms of wealth can "rot," literally. But this verb (*sēpō*) is applied metaphorically to anything that is transitory. "Every work decays and ceases to exist, and the one who made it will pass away with it" (Sir. 14:19).[59]

Your gold and silver are corroded (5:3). Again, gold and silver cannot become corroded. But this language was commonly applied to all kinds of metals, including gold and silver (e.g., Sir. 29:10; Ep. Jer. 10) with the general sense "decay" (cf. Ezek. 24:6, 11, 12). Verses 2b–3a therefore characterize wealth as transitory and in process of decay.

Eat your flesh like fire (5:3). The same language is used to describe the judgment of God in Judith 16:17: "Woe to the nations that rise up against my people! The Lord Almighty will take vengeance on them in the day of judgment; he will send fire and worms into their flesh; they shall weep in pain forever."

You have hoarded wealth in the last days (5:3). We could also translate "for the last days"; some interpreters think that James may simply be describing the way the

▶ The Problem With Wealth

James does not make clear why the transitory nature of wealth will bring judgment to these rich people. But Old Testament and Jewish teaching can fill in the gap. (1) The hoarding of wealth was often thought to manifest a sinful tendency to focus on this world instead of the world to come. See, for example, Ezekiel 7:19: "They will throw their silver into the streets, and their gold will be an unclean thing. Their silver and gold will not be able to save them in the day of the LORD's wrath. They will not satisfy their hunger or fill their stomachs with it, for it has made them stumble into sin." Jesus, reflecting this tradition, warns people about focusing on "earthly treasures" at the expense of "heavenly treasure," thereby indicating the tendency of the heart (cf. Matt. 6:19–21).

(2) James may also be implying a more specific condemnation. Sirach, a book that has many parallels with the teaching of James, suggests a connection between wealth and a failure to help the poor in language similar to what we find here in James: "Help the poor for the commandment's sake, and in their need do not send them away empty-handed. Lose your silver for the sake of a brother or a friend, and do not let it rust under a stone and be lost. Lay up your treasure according to the commandments of the Most High, and it will profit you more than gold" (Sir. 29:9–11). So James might think that the rich are to be condemned because they have hoarded wealth for themselves while others have gone without the basic necessities of life.

wealthy are saving money for the future. But the "last days" is a phrase that New Testament writers use against the background of Jewish apocalyptic to denote the age of salvation. The "last days" begin with the coming of Messiah and, in a twist on the Jewish apocalyptic scheme, will be climaxed in a second coming of the Messiah. Thus, the period of the church is "the last days."[60] What James suggests is that the hoarding of wealth is all the more culpable because it is occurring in the age of salvation, with the Day of Judgment imminent.

The wages you failed to pay the workmen (5:4). The Greek text for the verb translated "failed to pay" in the NIV is uncertain. Some manuscripts have a form of the verb *apostereō* ("defraud") while others have *aphystereō*, "withhold." But the former is more likely because the verb occurs elsewhere in the Bible in just this sense. See especially Malachi 3:5: "'So I will come near to you for judgment. I will be quick to testify against sorcerers, adulterers and perjurers, against those who defraud laborers of their wages, who oppress the widows and the fatherless, and deprive aliens of justice, but do not fear me,' says the LORD Almighty." James might again be influenced by Leviticus 19 in his selection of this particular example, for 19:13 reads, "Do not defraud your neighbor or rob him. Do not hold back the wages of a hired man overnight."

Are crying out against you (5:4). We are reminded of Cain's blood, "crying out" for justice (Gen. 4:10). But even more pertinent may be Deuteronomy 24:14–15: "Do not take advantage of a hired man who is poor and needy, whether he is a brother Israelite or an alien living in one of your towns. Pay him his wages each day before sunset, because he is poor and is counting on it. Otherwise he may cry to the LORD against you, and you will be guilty of sin." The language of "crying out" is often used in the Bible when God's people plead with God for deliverance from their oppressors.[61]

The Lord Almighty (5:4). "Almighty" translates a word that means "armies" (*sabaōth*). The language pictures God as the powerful leader of a great army, usually the heavenly hosts. It may not be coincidence that Isaiah uses this title of God when he describes the judgment God will bring on his people for their oppression of the poor (Isa. 5:9).

The day of slaughter (5:5). The Greek of this phrase does not occur in the LXX, but the Hebrew equivalent is found as a reference to the Day of the Lord in Isaiah 30:25. It also occurs in a similar way in *1 Enoch* 90:4. Almost certainly, then, James refers to the time of final judgment.

You have condemned and murdered innocent men (5:6). James's accusation reflects a widespread Old Testament/Jewish tradition about the sinfulness of rich people in using their wealth and influence to defraud the poor and to deprive them of their living. In Wisdom of Solomon 2:6–20, for instance, the rich are pictured as living luxuriously with no thought of tomorrow, oppressing "the righteous man" (2:12) and condemning them "to a shameful death" (2:20).[62] To withhold wages from a working man is, in effect, to murder him, as Sirach says: "To take away a neighbor's living is to commit murder" (Sir. 34:22).

The Need for Patient Endurance (5:7–11)

The contribution of this paragraph to the argument of the letter is debated. Some interpreters note parallels between this paragraph and 1:2–12 (notably God's blessing on those who "endure") and think that James here begins the conclusion of the letter. But the biblical background suggests a closer relationship with 5:1–6. Several Old Testament texts—Psalm 37 is perhaps the best example—exhort the oppressed people of God to take comfort from the fact that God will judge the wicked. So James turns from portraying the terrible fate that the wicked rich, who are oppressing the righteous, will face on the Day of the Lord to encouraging God's people to endure faithfully in light of the nearness of that Day.

The Lord's coming (5:7). "Coming" translates *parousia*, a word that is applied throughout the New Testament to the appearance of Christ in glory at the end of history. *Parousia* basically means "presence" and was used in secular Greek to depict the "arrival" of a king or dignitary.[63]

The farmer waits for the land to yield its valuable crop and how patient he is for the autumn and spring rains (5:7). In Palestine, the growth of crops was particularly dependent on the rain that came in late autumn and early spring.[64] Note, for example, Deuteronomy 11:14, where God, in response to his people's obedience, promises: "Then I will send rain on your land in its season, both autumn and spring rains, so that you may gather in your grain, new wine and oil." Every passage in which the language of "early and late rains" appears in the Old Testament affirms God's faithfulness to his people.[65] James's readers may well have detected an "echo" of this faithfulness theme in the illustration here.

▶

MODERN
HARVEST NEAR
THE DEAD SEA

Don't grumble against each other (5:9). The word "grumble" translates a word (*stenazō*) that often connotes the frustration of God's people at the oppression that they are suffering. Exodus 2:23 is a classic example: "During that long period, the king of Egypt died. The Israelites groaned in their slavery and cried out, and their cry for help because of their slavery went up to God." James, of course, here prohibits believers from grumbling against each other. But his use of this word may hint at the fact that their impatience with one another is the product of the persecution they are enduring.

As an example of patience in the face of suffering (5:10). Citing examples of endurance under the pressure of persecution became a standard Jewish means of encouragement in the wake of the Maccabean revolt in the early second century B.C. The Seleucid king of that era, Antiochus IV Epiphanes, sought to eradicate the Jewish faith by prohibiting circumcision, possession of the Torah, and other Jewish customs. Many Jews refused to abandon their faith and were severely persecuted as a result. Books such as 2 Maccabees celebrate the faithfulness and endurance of these martyrs as means of encouraging God's people. The word translated "example" (*hypodeigma*) occurs in some of these traditions (cf. 2 Macc. 6:28; 4 Macc. 17:23). Note especially 4 Maccabees 9:8: "For we, through this severe suffering and endurance, shall have the prize of virtue and be with God." Hebrews 11:35–37 refers to some of these same martyrs, and James here alludes briefly to this same tradition.

We consider blessed those who have persevered (5:11). James may again be reflecting a dependence on the Maccabean martyr tradition. At the opening of his book, after introducing Eleazar, his seven brothers, and their mother as model martyrs, the author of *4 Maccabees* says, "It is fitting for me to praise for their virtues those who, with their mother, died for the sake of nobility and goodness, but I would call them blessed for the honor in which they are held" (*4 Macc. 1:10*).

You have heard of Job's perseverance (5:11). The canonical book of Job does not put much emphasis on the heroic perseverance of Job; although he does tenaciously cling to his faith in God despite the best efforts of his "friends." But the noncanonical *Testament of Job* puts much greater stress on this element of Job's response, praising him for his "endurance" (*T. Job* 1:5) and having him remind his children that "patience is better than anything." The date of this book is uncertain and may even have been redacted by Christian scribes.[66] But the tradition found in the book may predate James.

What the Lord finally brought about (5:11). The NIV suggests that James refers at this point to the blessings God eventually restored to Job at the end of the book. But the Greek is ambiguous, referring more vaguely to "the end [or purpose] of the Lord." Nevertheless the NIV translation is probably justified, for the closest parallels to James's wording in intertestamental literature have a similar reference.[67]

Concluding Exhortations (5:12–20)

New Testament letters often end with a focus on prayer. James is no exception. The power of prayer in all circumstances, but especially in times of illness, is the focus of these verses. But James begins with a brief prohibition of oaths (5:12) and ends with a fitting encouragement to believers to bring back fellow Christians who may be leaving the straight path of the faith (5:19–20).

Do not swear (5:12). James does not refer to uncouth speech but to invoking God's name as the guarantee of truth or a future course of action. Such oaths are apparently being abused in James's day. Intertestamental writers warn against taking oaths too often.[68] James has apparently modeled his prohibition on the similar teaching of Jesus that we find in Matthew 5:34–37. Perhaps Leviticus 19 is also exerting some influence on James, for verse 12 in that chapter reads, "Do not swear falsely by my name and so profane the name of your God. I am the LORD."

Is any one of you sick? (5:14). "Sick" translates a Greek word (*astheneō*) that means "to be weak." Some interpreters think the weakness to which James refers is perhaps spiritual rather than physical. But, as we have seen throughout the letter, James is strongly influenced by the teaching of Jesus. In the Gospels, *astheneō* consistently refers to physical weakness, such as an illness.

The elders of the church (5:14). The office of elder in the early church may well have been modeled on the elders of the synagogue. They were the spiritual leaders of the local congregations of believers.[69]

right ▶

JARS FOR OIL

Small jars discovered at Masada.

Anoint him with oil (5:14). Why does James encourage the elders to anoint the sick person with oil? One possibility is

that the oil will have had a medicinal value. Oil was widely used in the ancient world in cases of illness. Galen, the most famous ancient physician, recommended oil as "the best of all remedies for paralysis."[70] Note that the good Samaritan, when he came across the injured man, "bandaged his wounds, pouring on oil and wine" (Luke 10:34). Yet we have no evidence that oil was considered a panacea (note that Galen stipulates its usefulness in cases of paralysis). So it seems unlikely that James recommends oil as the natural remedy for illness in general.

The anointing is more likely, then, to have a symbolic value. In the Old Testament anointing especially often symbolizes the setting apart of a thing or person for God's special attention or use. Typical is Exodus 28:41: "After you put these clothes on your brother Aaron and his sons, anoint and ordain them. Consecrate them so that they might serve me as priests." To be sure, the Greek verb in the LXX of many of these passages is *chriō* rather than the *aleiphō*, which James uses

here. But *aleiphō* can be used in this same way (see Ex. 40:15; Num. 3:3), and James probably avoids *chriō* because in the New Testament it has ceased to refer clearly to a physical action. James wants the elders to perform an actual physical anointing as a means of assuring the person who is ill that he or she is being held up in a special way for God's attention in prayer.

And the prayer offered in faith will make the sick person well (5:15). A few zealous Christians insist that God wants to heal his people through prayer and that any recourse to medicine betrays a lack of faith in God's power. But James almost certainly shares the view enunciated by Sirach:

> Honor physicians for their services,
>   for the Lord created them;
> for their gift of healing comes from the
>   Most High,
>   and they are rewarded by the king.
> The skill of physicians makes them
>   distinguished,
>   and the sensible will not despise
>   them.
> The Lord created medicines out of
>   the earth,
>   and the sensible do not despise
>   them.[71]

He prayed earnestly that it would not rain (5:17). Elijah's prayer is found in 1 Kings 17–18. This text does not explicitly claim that Elijah prayed for the drought. But 1 Kings 18:42 does picture him praying for the drought to end, and

it is a legitimate inference that he prayed for its onset as well. Note also that a few Jewish texts associate the drought with Elijah's praying.[72]

Cover over a multitude of sins (5:20). James alludes to Proverbs 10:12: "Hatred stirs up dissension, but love covers over all wrongs." In Proverbs, "cover" refers to the overlooking of the sins that people commit against us. But, since "cover" here in James is parallel with "save from death," it seems to refer to God's forgiveness. There is some evidence, based on the use of this same text in 1 Peter 4:8, that this language had become a proverbial way of referring to divine forgiveness.

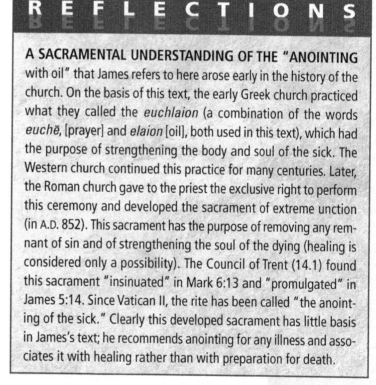

REFLECTIONS

A SACRAMENTAL UNDERSTANDING OF THE "ANOINTING with oil" that James refers to here arose early in the history of the church. On the basis of this text, the early Greek church practiced what they called the *euchlaion* (a combination of the words *euchē*, [prayer] and *elaion* [oil], both used in this text), which had the purpose of strengthening the body and soul of the sick. The Western church continued this practice for many centuries. Later, the Roman church gave to the priest the exclusive right to perform this ceremony and developed the sacrament of extreme unction (in A.D. 852). This sacrament has the purpose of removing any remnant of sin and of strengthening the soul of the dying (healing is considered only a possibility). The Council of Trent (14.1) found this sacrament "insinuated" in Mark 6:13 and "promulgated" in James 5:14. Since Vatican II, the rite has been called "the anointing of the sick." Clearly this developed sacrament has little basis in James's text; he recommends anointing for any illness and associates it with healing rather than with preparation for death.

ANNOTATED BIBLIOGRAPHY

Davids, Peter. *The Epistle of James.* NIGTC. Grand Rapids: Eerdmans, 1982.

Excellent commentary on the Greek text, particularly strong on Jewish backgrounds.

Dibelius, Martin. *A Commentary on the Epistle of James*, rev. by H. Greeven. Philadelphia: Fortress, 1976.

Classic work, very good on backgrounds but weak on literary structure.

Johnson, L. T. *The Letter of James.* AB. Garden City, N.Y.: Doubleday, 1995.

The best recent commentary, with excellent material on Greco-Roman background and structure.

Laws, Sophie. *A Commentary on the Epistle of James.* New York: Harper & Row, 1980.

Classic exposition of the English text.

Martin, R. P. *James.* WBC. Waco, Tex.: Word, 1988.

Detailed commentary on the Greek text, with a particular slant on the Jewish background.

Moo, D. J. *The Letter of James.* Pillar. Grand Rapids: Eerdmans, 2000.

Exposition of the English text.

CHAPTER NOTES

Main Text Notes

1. Acts 12:17; 15:13; 21:18; cf. Gal. 1:19; 2:9, 12.
2. See esp. Hegesippus (and cf. R. B. Ward, "James of Jerusalem in the First Two Centuries," *ANRW* 2.26.1 [1992]: 799–810).
3. On the issue of James's family background, see esp. R. Bauckham, *Jude and the Relatives of Jesus in the Early Church* (Edinburgh: T. & T. Clark, 1990), 125–30.
4. See, e.g., Elsa Tamez, *The Scandalous Message of James: Faith Without Works Is Dead* (New York: Crossroad, 1990).
5. *A Commentary on the Epistle of James*, ed. H. Greeven (Hermeneia; Philadelphia: Fortress, 1976).
6. See, e.g., W. R. Baker, *Personal Speech-Ethics in the Epistle of James* (Tubingen: Mohr, 1995), 7–12.
7. Ezek. 47:13; *Pss. Sol.* 17:26–28; see also Matt. 19:28; Rev. 7:4–8; 21:12.
8. For further information on "wisdom," see esp. Ben Witherington, III, *Jesus the Sage: The Pilgrimage of Wisdom* (Minneapolis: Fortress, 1994), 3–116.
9. Ps. 12:2 (LXX, where it is 11:3); Hos. 10:2 (LXX).
10. See, e.g., Sir. 15:11–20; *b. Men.* 99b; *b. Sanh.* 59b.
11. See *Gen. Rab.* 9:7; *b. Yoma* 69b.
12. Philo, *Husbandry* 103.
13. Philo, *Alleg. Interp.* 2.33.
14. Ibid., 2.33.
15. Prov. 10:19; 15:1; 17:27–28; Sir. 5:9–6:1.
16. See, e.g., Prov. 8:20; Isa. 1:21; Jer. 9:24; Tobit 1:3.
17. Simeon b. Gamaliel, *m. Abot.* 1:17.
18. Philo, *Spec. Laws* 1.315.
19. See Rom. 2:11; Eph. 6:9; Col. 3:25; related words are found in Acts 10:34; James 2:9; 1 Peter 1:17; on the Hebrew idea of partiality, see, e.g., Lev. 19:15; Deut. 1:17; Ps. 82:2; Prov. 28:21; Mal. 1:8.
20. See also Matt. 21:21; Mark 11:23; Acts 10:20; Rom. 4:20; 14:23; Jude 22.
21. E.g., Ps. 69:32; Isa. 29:19; 61:1; Amos 2:7.
22. Philo, *Posterity* 101–2.
23. See esp. L. T. Johnson, "The Use of Leviticus 19 in the Letter of James," *JBL* 101 (1982): 391–401.
24. Augustine, *Letter to Heironymum* 4.
25. See also *b. Hor.* 8b; *b. Shab.* 70b; 1QS 8:16; *T. Asher* 2:5–10; Philo, *Alleg. Interp.* 3.241.
26. Vaticanus, B; see also Luke 18:20; Rom. 13:9.
27. Judg. 6:23; 1 Sam. 25:35; 2 Kings 5:19; Mark 5:34; Luke 7:50; 8:48; 24:36; John 20:19; Acts 16:36.
28. Josephus, *Ag. Ap.* 2.40 §284.
29. Cf. 1 Cor. 8:4–6; Gal. 3:20; Eph. 4:6; 1 Tim. 2:5.
30. MM, 676.
31. Philo, *Worse* 140.
32. Cf., e.g., Ps. 105:6; Jer. 33:26; cf. Gal. 3:16; Heb. 2:16.
33. Cf. Philo, *Virtues* 216; Josephus, *Ant.* 1.154–57; *Jub.* 11–12.

34. The translation "friend" in many English translations of these verses is a paraphrase of a Hebrew construction that means "one loved."

35. *Jub.* 19:9; 20:20; Philo, *Sobriety* 56; *Abraham* 273; *T. Ab.*, passim.

36. See esp. R. B. Ward, "The Works of Abraham: James 2:14–26," *HTR* 61 (1968): 283–90.

37. Philo, *Posterity* 88.

38. Sophocles, *Antigone* 477.

39. Aristotle, *Questiones Mechanica* 5.

40. E.g., Pseudo-Aristotle, *De mundo* 6; frequently in Philo.

41. Philo, *Creation* 83–86.

42. Philo, *Alleg. Interp.* 3.224.

43. L. E. Elliott-Binns, "The Meaning of '*YLH* in Jas. III.5," *NTS* 2 (1995): 48–50.

44. E.g., Philo, *Spec. Laws* 4.110–16; Acts 11:6.

45. Prov. 26:28; cf. Hermas, *Mandates* 2:3.

46. *Gen. Rab.* 24 (on Gen. 5:1).

47. Epictetus, *Diss.* 2.20.18–19.

48. Aristotle, *Politics* 5.3.

49. See esp. R. P. Martin, *James* (WBC; Waco, Tex.: Word, 1988), 144.

50. Epictetus, *Diss.* 3.13.9.

51. E.g., Ex. 20:5; 34:14; Zech. 8:2.

52. E.g., Lev. 21:17, 21, 23; Isa. 29:13; 58:2; Ezek. 40:46; Heb. 7:19.

53. Num. 31:23; 2 Chron. 29:15; Isa. 66:17.

54. Cf. Prov. 10:23; Eccl. 7:6; cf. Sir. 27:13.

55. See, e.g., *Pss. Sol.* 12:3; *T. Gad* 3:3; cf. also 2 Cor. 12:20; 1 Peter 2:1.

56. Hermas, *Mandates* 2; cf. James 4:8.

57. See Sophie Laws, *A Commentary on the Epistle of James* (New York: Harper & Row, 1980), 194.

58. See esp. *1 En.* 94–105.

59. See also Job 16:7; 19:20; 33:21; 40:12; Ps. 37:36; Ezek. 17:9; Ep. Jer. 71.

60. See, e.g., Acts 2:17; 2 Tim. 3:1; Heb. 1:2; 2 Peter 3:3.

61. Ex. 2:23; 1 Sam. 9:16; 2 Chron. 33:13; cf. *3 Macc.* 5:7.

62. See also Ps. 10:8–9; 37:32; Amos 2:6; 5:12; Mic. 2:2, 6–9; 3:1–3, 9–12; 6:9–16.

63. Cf. 1 Cor. 16:7; 2 Cor. 10:10; Phil. 2:12.

64. D. Baly, *The Geography of the Bible* (New York: Harper & Row, 1974), 50–51.

65. Cf. also Jer. 5:24; Hos. 6:3; Joel 2:23; Zech. 10:1.

66. See C. Hass, "Job's Perseverance in the Testament of Job," in *Studies on the Testament of Job*, eds. M. A. Knibb and P. W. van der Horst (SNTSMS 66; Cambridge: Cambridge Univ. Press, 1989), 117–18.

67. Cf. *T. Gad* 7:4; *T. Benj.* 4:1; cf. Heb. 13:7.

68. Sir. 23:9, 11; Philo, *Decalogue* 84–95.

69. Cf. Acts 11:30; 14:23; 15:2; 20:17; 21:18; 1 Tim. 5:17.

70. Galen, *De simplicitate medicamentum* 2.

71. Sir. 38:1–4.

72. Sir. 48:2–3; 2 Esd. 7:109.

Sidebar and Chart Notes

A-1. See, e.g., Isa. 43:9; 45:25; 50:8.

A-2. An introduction and translation can be found in James H. Charlesworth, ed., *The Old Testament Pseudepigrapha*, vol. 1 (Garden City, N.Y.: Doubleday, 1983), while the classic commentary is R. H. Charles, *The Testaments of the Twelve Patriarchs* (2 vols.; Oxford: Clarendon, 1908).

A-3. On this, see esp. L. T. Johnson, "James 3:13–4:10 and the *Topos PERI FQONOU*," *NovT* 25 (1983): 327–47.

CREDITS FOR PHOTOS AND MAPS

Arnold, Clinton E. . . . . p. 8
Claycombe, Hugh . . . . p. 56
Dunn, Cheryl (for Talbot Bible Lands) . . . . pp. 22, 52
Franz, Gordon . . . . p. 36
Isachar, Hanan . . . . pp. 58, 94
King, Jay . . . . pp. 18, 29
Kohlenberger, John R. III . . . . pp. 5, 89, 90–91
Konstas, Ioannis . . . . p. 74
Radovan, Zev . . . . pp. 4(2), 7, 8, 12, 15, 16, 20, 28,
42, 62, 70, 80, 96, 98, 104, 116
Ritmeyer, Leen . . . . pp. 49, 61
Tabernacle . . . . pp. 31, 45, 51, 53(2), 54, 55, 59, 64
University of Michigan . . . . pp. 21, 34, 102
Zondervan Image Archive (Neal Bierling) . . . . pp. 2–3, 6(2), 9, 24, 39, 51,
77, 86–87, 105(2), 110, 114

ALSO AVAILABLE

Matthew — Michael J. Wilkins

Mark — David E. Garland

Luke — Mark L. Strauss

John — Andreas J. Köstenberger

Acts — Clinton E. Arnold

Romans
Galatians — Douglas J. Moo, Ralph P. Martin, Julie L. Wu

1 & 2 Corinthians — David W. J. Gill, Moyer V. Hubbard

Ephesians
Philippians
Colossians
Philemon — Clinton E. Arnold, Frank S. Thielman, S. M. Baugh

1 & 2 Thessalonians
1 & 2 Timothy
Titus — Jeffrey A. D. Weima, S. M. Baugh

Hebrews
James — George H. Guthrie, Douglas J. Moo

1 & 2 Peter
1, 2, & 3 John
Jude — Peter H. Davids, Douglas J. Moo, Robert W. Yarbrough

Revelation — Mark W. Wilson

ALSO AVAILABLE

CPSIA information can be obtained at www.ICGtesting.com
Printed in the USA
LVOW03s1932250615

443851LV00004B/12/P